The Internet of Money Volume T

Andreas M. Antonopoulos

The Internet of Money Volume Three

A collection of talks by Andreas M. Antonopoulos

aantonop.com

Dedicated to the bitcoin community

Talks by Andreas M. Antonopoulos

https://aantonop.com/

@aantonop

Cover Design

Kathrine Smith: http://kathrinevsmith.com/

Transcription and Editing

Janine Römer, Jessica Levesque, Pamela Morgan

First print: **December 15, 2019**

Second print: **February 10, 2020**

Third print: **November 25, 2020**

Errata Submissions: errata@merklebloom.com

Licensing Requests: licensing@merklebloom.com

General: info@merklebloom.com

ISBN: 978-1-947910-17-1

Table of Contents

Praise for The Internet of Money

Cryptocurrencies may change the world more than the Internet did and most people are not aware. Andreas does a great job at explaining these otherwise complicated issues in a way that is easy and even fun to understand. — Wences Casares, *CEO of Xapo*

One is hard pressed to find a field more multidisciplinary than that of cryptocurrency. This makes it devilishly hard to explain and understand, because even an expert in one field is a beginner in many other relevant domains. Yet this is what Andreas M. Antonopoulos achieves with The Internet of Money series: explaining cryptocurrency in terms accessible to all. In this volume, he moves deftly between topics ranging from economics to computer science, from governance to online communities. He offers something for everyone, no matter where they are starting from. — Jill Carlson, *Co-founder, Open Money Initiative*

What does it mean for the internet to have an uncensorable value transfer layer? We don't know yet! We only know it will be revolutionary. While we can't yet see into the foggy future, there is no one better than Andreas Antonopoulos at illuminating the road ahead. You may not agree with all of his predictions and opinions, but you can't ignore them. — Evan Van Ness, *Week in Ethereum News*

As a professional blockchain instructor, I often find myself making use of Andreas's material. Many of the talks transcribed in this volume of The Internet of Money have already proven themselves to be valuable resources in the classroom.These materials help students navigate the maze of blockchain options and understand the impact of using blockchain tech both for themselves and for customers of the businesses they build.

Andreas has a real skill for presenting these concepts, not just in a non-technical and easily understood fashion, but in a way that really communicates the importance and human impact of these technologies.

— Hannah Rosenberg, *Managing Director of The Blockhain Institute and Adjunct Teaching Associate at UIC's College of Business Administration*

Andreas M. Antonopoulos doesn't simply lament that we can do better, he details the tools we have available and the route we have already underway. The Internet of Money brings us all together through the telling of a familiar absurdity that is our past and present, while teaching about the future now ahead thanks to a technology that will inspire, infuriate, and liberate for generations to come. — Joshua McDougall, *Director, C4*

Andreas M. Antonopoulos' latest work offers knowledge that will broaden your perspective of and provide greater depth to your understanding of Bitcoin. Whether you are a Bitcoin newbie or a long-time enthusiast, Andreas' talks are energetic, spontaneous, eye-opening and entertaining all at once. In each chapter you will discover something new. — Anita Posch, *Podcast Host, Author of "Bitcoin & Co. Kryptowährungen sicher kaufen, verwalten und verwahren" and Board Member of "Bitcoin Austria"*

For over seven years, I have been honored to fight alongside my friend Andreas Antonopoulos against political currency and for monetary sovereignty as applied through cryptography, freedom of speech and sound money. I cannot think of a more important battle because this is a fight with only two possible outcomes: Either control of their own lives by the individuals themselves or control of the people and their lives by political and economic elitists. — Trace Mayer, *Host of The Bitcoin Knowledge Podcast*

In the '80s most people didn't think they had a need for one computer, let alone the ability to connect it to others, but a select few shared their dreams of an information-driven and connected future. Andreas's latest instalment of Internet of Money strikes the same chord when describing why blockchains matter in a decentralized future: hopeful, prescient, visionary. — Michael Perklin, *President, C4*

With eloquence and passion, Andreas makes the case for the transformative power of decentralized technologies. There is nobody on the planet who can convey these concepts with as much accessibility without oversimplifying the technology. And he never forgets the *why* behind it all.

This book is a fantastic collection of Andreas' best talks. A must-read for anyone interested in the radical future ahead of us. — Brian Fabian Crain, *Co-Host Epicenter Podcast & CEO Chorus One*

Preface

By Andreas M. Antonopoulos

When I started my journey in bitcoin, I never thought it would lead to this. This book is like an abridged diary of my discovery of bitcoin and open blockchains, delivered through a series of talks.

Over these past seven years, I have delivered more than 200 talks to audiences across the world, recorded more than 400 podcast episodes, answered several hundred questions, participated in more than 200 interviews for radio, print and TV, appeared in eight documentaries and written two technical books called *Mastering Bitcoin* and *Mastering Ethereum*. Almost all of this work is available, for free, under open-source licenses, online. The talks included in this book are only a small sample of my work, selected by the editorial team to provide a glimpse into bitcoin and open blockchains, their uses, and their impact on the future.

Each of these talks was delivered to a live audience, without slides or any visual aides, and was mostly improvised. While I have a topic in mind before each talk, a lot of my inspiration comes from the energy and interaction with the audience. From talk to talk, the topics evolve as I try out new ideas, see the reaction and develop them further. Eventually, some ideas that start as a single sentence evolve, over several talks, into an entire topic.

This process of discovery is not perfect, of course. My talks are littered with minor factual errors. I recite dates, events, numbers, and technical details from memory and often get them wrong. In this book, my off-the-cuff errors, malapropisms, and verbal tics have been cleaned up by the editors. What remains is the essence of each presentation — how I wish it had been delivered, rather than a transcript of the actual delivery. But, with that cleanup there is also a price to pay. What is missing is the reaction and energy of the audience, the tone of my sentences, the spontaneous giggles from me and the people in the room. For all of that you have to watch the videos which are linked in Appendix C, *Video Links* of the book.

This book and my work over the past seven years is about more than bitcoin. These talks reflect my worldview, my political ideas and my hopes, as well as my technical fascination and my unabashed geekiness. They summarize my enthusiasm about this technology and the astonishing future that I envision. This vision starts with bitcoin, a quirky cypherpunk experiment which unleashes a ripple of innovation, creating "The Internet of Money" and radically transforming society.

Note from the Editors

Almost the entire bitcoin and open blockchain community knows of Andreas's contributions. In addition to his written and audio work, he's a highly sought-after public speaker, lauded for consistently delivering innovative, thought-provoking, engaging talks. This book represents only a small sampling of Andreas's work in the bitcoin and blockchain industry over the years. With so much content, simply deciding which talks to include was an arduous task. We selected these specific talks because they fit the criteria of the book; we could easily have included dozens more. This book is Volume Three in The Internet of Money series, we hope to publish another volume soon.

We began this book project with a vision: to provide an easy-to-read, short-story style overview of why bitcoin matters, of why so many of us are excited about it. We wanted something we could share with family, friends, and co-workers that they might actually read: a compendium that they could pick up for five minutes, no-commitment, or explore for a few hours. It needed to be engaging, with real-world analogies to make the tech understandable. It needed to be inspirational, with a vision of how these things could positively impact humanity. It needed to be honest, acknowledging the shortcomings of our current systems and the technology itself.

Despite our best efforts, we're sure there are things we could improve and change. We've edited heavily in some places, for readability, while always trying to preserve the essence of the talk. We believe we've struck a good balance and we're pleased with the book as a whole. We hope you are too. If you've read Volumes One and Two, you'll notice some small changes in Volume Three, thanks to feedback we've received from readers just like you. You'll also notice that while most of the time we've used American spellings, other times we've used British English. Just like Andreas' our editing style has some British flare. If you have comments about editing, content, or suggestions about how we can make the book better, please email us at errata@merklebloom.com.

Tips to make your reading experience even better:

Each talk is intended to stand alone. There is no need to start at the beginning — although if you are unfamiliar with bitcoin, you may want to start at the first talk, "Introduction to the Internet of Money," to get an overview of the topic.

You'll find a robust index at the end of the book. One of the things we're most proud of is the index. We've worked hard to provide an index that will allow you to cross-reference and research themes and topics.

Introduction to The Internet of Money

The original video presentation of this talk was recorded at the *Internet Days ("Internetdagarna") Conference* in Stockholm, Sweden; November 2017. Video Link: https://aantonop.io/IntroTIOM

Technologies Transforming the World

Good evening, everyone! It's such a pleasure to be here. This is my first time in Sweden and I'm enjoying every moment of it… except for the weather. But other than that, fantastic!

It's so good to be at a conference about the internet, because I remember my first internet conference. It was in 1992. There were about one hundred people there; all of them were either computer scientists or computer science students. Despite the fact that we were telling everyone the entire world was about to change, no one believed us — at least, no one believed me because I was 19 years old, awkward and shy. But that experience taught me one thing: it taught me to trust my instincts. Because, in fact, the internet did change the world.

My second book series is called "The Internet of Money." The reason for that is because the technology I'm going to talk about today is about to transform the world in equal measure. It will also transform the internet itself.

New Invention, Old Narratives

Bitcoin is an invention launched on January 3, 2009 by an anonymous creator.   It was unleashed as an open-source project, built by a community of volunteers, and run as a peer-to-peer network. And then it was derided, laughed at, and ignored for the first five or six years. But not so much anymore.

People are beginning to pay attention, just like with the internet. Things that were previously unthinkable are now thinkable. People are beginning to notice that this is something more than what they are told.

And what are they told? They're told it's used only by derelicts. Drug dealers! Pornographers! Criminals!

Guess what? That's what they said at the first conference about the internet in 1992. They were wrong then and they are wrong now. Every time you meet someone like a dentist or a hairdresser who uses bitcoin, it undermines that silly narrative.

Bitcoin is a protocol, and what better stage than this one to talk about a protocol.

What is Money?

The moment you start talking about Bitcoin and thinking about Bitcoin, it brings up a very difficult question: what is money? Most of us have no idea what money is or how it works. It's one of those technologies that is so deeply embedded in our culture that it has become completely invisible to us. In fact, we don't even need to think about money unless it stops working. In some countries, money does stop working. And then everyone has interesting things to say about what money is.

What is money? At its very basic level, money isn't value. In fact, we use money to get things of value (products or services), but there is no value in the paper bills or coins themselves. Money isn't a construct of authority; although we seem to think that these days, because all of our money comes from certain authoritative sources. Some guy with a crown says "this is your money," therefore it's valuable. That's the authority it comes from.

But what if money could be created without an authority? What if money could be created simply through use? It turns out that what money really is, is a language. Money is a language that human beings created to express value to each other. As a language, it's one of the fundamental constructs of civilization that allows us to exceed what's known as the Dunbar number. The Dunbar number is the maximum number of individuals who can operate in a tribe on the basis of acquaintance. If you want two tribes to work together, you need some common bond. These bonds have included culture, language, religion, and money — these bonds are a fundamental construct that allow us to exceed the scale of a single tribe and engage in commerce with others on a greater scale.

Money is also, ironically, a system of control. Controlling money confers great power to those who control it. As a result, kings and governments have kept tight control over money, just as they used to keep tight control over religion, and for the same reasons.

Money as Pure Data

Now that has changed. On January 3, 2009 the world changed because some person(s) created a peer-to-peer protocol. They created a flat network with no central server, and this network is able to express money as a content type.

As internet professionals, you may understand what I mean when I say "money as a content type." I mean money that is expressed purely as data, and transmitted using any communication medium that can convey information.

As data, a bitcoin transaction doesn't need to be transmitted directly to the Bitcoin network, although that's a convenient way to do it. You could encode it in Skype emojis. You could write it up and put it in a Craigslist ad. You could post it on Facebook in the background of a picture of kittens playing with yarn.

Money has now become pure information, flowing on a network that is simultaneously uncensorable, open to anyone, neutral, and global. There are no borders on this new technology, just like there are no borders on the internet.

Everyone can access Bitcoin because it is not a product or a company. You do not need to register for an account. You simply download a client. As soon as you download that one application, you can join a global economy; that global economy is open to anyone of any race, religion, creed, ethnicity, age, and gender in the world.

For most people, this concept hasn't yet quite sunk in. The children born today may not know a world in which banks exist, a world in which paper money exists, any more than the young people in our industry today have any idea of what the world looked like before the internet. How many of you here remember libraries and looking up reference cards? Okay, you're over 40 years old. So am I. Gotcha!

The children born today may never drive a car, may never have a world without the internet; they will never know a world where banks control money and it is issued only by kings or nation states. Money will be an integral protocol of the internet as a content type that can be transmitted by anyone, anywhere.

But that's not enough. Let's make it more fun.

Money as an Autonomous System

Until now, every form of money had to have a person behind it. Previously, money could only be owned and managed by people, or people together forming an association - a legal fiction called the corporation. But Bitcoin is a protocol. Autonomous agents can use it to own and manage money themselves. No people required. Imagine a corporation with no directors, no shareholders, no employees, running entirely based on scripted machine learning or maybe just a few simple heuristic rules, that operates autonomously of any human action, managing budgets in the amounts of billions of dollars.

And at this point we have a split in the audience. Some people are thinking, *Oh no! That sounds terrible. What if it's a virus? What if it's intelligent ransomware that self-propagates and buys Amazon Web Service systems so that it can grow when it's successful? What if it starts running A/B testing on itself by hiring programmers to make it better?*

Yeah, all of that is going to happen. But what if it's an intelligent charity that detects the emergence of a natural disaster and then automatically and instantaneously diverts large funds directly to the people most in need without human intervention? And, unlike most charities today, 100% of the funds donated would go to those in need.

The world is about to change.

Self-driving cars? How about self-owning cars? Cars that are not owned by a corporation, but cars that *are* a corporation. Cars that pay for their electricity or gas, maintenance and leasing fees by giving rides to human beings who pay them in cryptocurrencies.

Imagine software as intelligent articles that propagate across the internet as content and expand their reach because people read them. As a result, they're able to buy more hosting services so they can further expand their reach.

Programmable Money

This is not the money of your grandparents' generation. It's not the money of your parents either. This is money that is fully programmable, scriptable, and with capabilities that can be finely tuned. You can specify who can access it and when, and how it can be dispersed. A whole new field called smart contracts has emerged, allowing us to program the behaviour of entire systems that can also manage money.

"Money" is such a narrow word to describe this, because we use things all the time that kind of look like money but aren't really money. What about loyalty points, tokens, subway cards, airline miles? What about the expression of a Justin Bieber fan with full access to the catalogue of music, as a token? What about all of the other brands that can be turned into tokens and made into a global exchangeable system directly on the internet through this protocol?

On January 3, 2009 the world changed. Since then, more than a thousand other cryptocurrencies have been created using the same recipe, almost all of them open-source. They're expanding in all directions, exploring every possible niche of this ecosystem, every tiny variation in capabilities and features, creating new markets, raising funds for thousands of start-ups around the world. Thousands of software engineers and developers are training to use this technology. The internet itself is changing very rapidly. Now we have autonomous agents that are using money on the internet; these are, in many cases, beyond the control of any jurisdiction.

Intranet Blockchains

What are the large corporations going to do with this new magical, open, decentralized, neutral, borderless, censorship-resistant network?

They're going to say, "Great! We'd like that... but could you take out the open, decentralized, neutral, borderless, censorship-resistant properties and package it with a service-level agreement (SLA), a twelve-month license, and control? Control for us." They will take the internet and they will make intranets. They will make closed gardens of boring, stale content that is fundamentally insecure and sits in the backyard of corporations adding a tiny bit of value. It will be outside the participation of the global community, insulated from the wave of innovation that is happening all around us.

They will create intranets, they will claim victory, they will turn around and they will say, "We invented Blockchain." They will be wrong and they will fail.

Distributed Consensus

The real exciting thing about this technology is not a blockchain. A blockchain is a database artefact created out of this protocol. No, the real excitement comes from the ability to achieve distributed consensus among parties that don't trust each other, across great distances, without any central party, authority, or intermediary.

That consensus from the outside looks chaotic, messy, and weird. Well, everyone in this room already knows something that is open, flat, weird, and not understood by corporations: the internet. We already did it once, we're going to do it again. This time, we're going to bring the entire world with us.

Reversing the Trend of Financial Exclusion

In the background of this grand story, there is another story that's playing out. After 25 years of the internet, it still takes three to five days to send money from here to a country outside of Europe using banks. It will still cost you $30-40 to send money and that's only if the country you're sending it to isn't a poor country. If it is, that transaction will cost far more and take far longer. A giant network of centralized, closed, corrupt systems that are sucking money out of the poorest people on this planet.

Today there are three-and-a-half to four billion people on the internet; however, just over one billion people among them have banking and full access to financial services. Imagine what happens if you bring banking as an app to everyone who has a $20 Android smartphone.

This is going to change the world faster than the spread of cell phones. Imagine a $20 Android smartphone landing in a village in Kenya. But now it's no longer just a communications device, it's a bank. Not a bank account, but a bank. It can *wire* and receive funds from anyone and from anywhere in the world. It can do lending or receive loans for a mortgage, to buy seeds for a field, to bring disaster relief. It can directly connect to billions of people on this planet, bypassing traditional banking completely. We can do this within the next ten years.

The world will radically transform when you bring the capability of broad economic inclusion to everyone in this world. You might think that banks want to do this. You'd be wrong. It's not really profitable serving people who have little money, little connectivity, no access to ID, in oppressed countries with terrible governments. Also, in most of those countries, banks *are* criminals and criminal organisations. Or really quite indistinguishable from the local mob.

We Won't Ask For Permission

So how do we fix that? Up to now the approach for all of these technologies, whether it was PayPal or any of the others we've seen slowly emerge in financial technology, was to carefully and politely ask for permission. Bitcoin is not asking for permission. We forgot to do that. And we will proceed in (un)banking the entire world without asking for anyone's permission.

The Bitcoin protocol is now spreading. If this one gets shut down, a 14-year-old with a copy of my book *Mastering Bitcoin* can rebuild it in a weekend, in any programming language, and launch it again with a new name. Again and again until we succeed.

The world is now connected. Finance is now an application and money is a content type. Welcome to our new planet.

Thank you.

Universal Access to Basic Finance

The original video presentation of this talk was recorded at the
CryptoCompare Digital Asset Summit in London, England; June 2019.
Video Link: https://aantonop.io/UniversalAccess

The Future of Cryptocurrency and Finance

Today the topic of my talk is Universal Access to Basic Finance. At the
moment, we are at a crossroads. We are having a great debate about the
future of cryptocurrency and finance. A lot of people are expressing some
very strong opinions, myself included. The backdrop to all of this, are the
people who aren't in this room and will never be in a room like this.

Banking the Unbanked

In 2013, I visited the beautiful country of Argentina for the first time,
and gave a talk in Buenos Aires. It completely changed the direction and
trajectory of my involvement in Bitcoin and open blockchains. For the first
time, I didn't need to explain the "why" of Bitcoin, open blockchains, and
freedom in finance. Everybody there was interested in only one question:
how do I get involved right now? Because the why was already obvious to
people from Argentina.

While I was there, someone came up to me and said, "You have inspired
me today. I was almost too terrified to come to this conference. I am afraid
of what might happen if our government changes again. My grandparents
were kidnapped by the previous regime. We didn't see them for months and
thought they had been thrown out of an airplane."

Think about that for a second.

When we talk about financial inclusion, we talk about the banked and
unbanked. But we have no clue, from our position of privilege, what this
really means. What that Argentinian said shook me to the core. Every year
since 2013, I've had conversations like that. When I talk about these stories
in public, even more people come to me and say, "I hear you, because that is
my story too."

The Meaning of "Unbanked"

What does it mean to be unbanked? The World Bank defines unbanked as 2.5 billion people who have absolutely no access to financial services... and live in cash-based societies. Conveniently, they only count heads of household. Spouses and children are unimportant in this calculation; only the primary earners matter. Yet we know that in the vast majority of the world, day-to-day household finances are controlled by women. But they are not counted as the head of household.

To be unbanked is not to simply live in a cash-based society. To be unbanked is to lack connectivity to the world, to lack the ability to participate in trade and commerce, to be unable to get a job and find people who want your services. To be unbanked is to struggle to build a more secure future for your children. It is to be condemned to poverty.

When we look at those conditions, we think, 'They don't have money, that's why they're unbanked.' Wrong. Absolutely wrong. They don't have access, documentation, or the necessary literacy to fill in an application form. Sometimes they don't even have the clothes, shoes, or appearance to be able to enter a bank without being kicked out by a security guard. That is what it means to be unbanked.

The Cost of Financial Exclusion

What is the cost of financial exclusion? It creates enormous poverty around the world just so we can persist in this petty, bourgeois idea that as long as every participant must prove their identity, we can track every transaction through this surveillance system and end crime. By believing in that false idea of safety through totalitarian control, we condemn billions of people to poverty. Not just 2.5 billion, but many more.

We talk about financial inclusion from the perspective of the rich and privileged world we live in. The world I live in. As an American citizen, I can not only open a bank account, but I can also trade in multiple currencies without restrictions and access investment opportunities all around the world. I have access to stable currencies that hopefully won't destroy themselves overnight, taking my entire savings with them. I have access to institutions that, at least most of the time, are not actively stealing my money or rapidly destroying the currency in order to pay off their debt through hyperinflation, leading to financial collapse. How many people have that? Everyone in this room, probably.

But if you count people around the world with access to that level of financial services, it is maybe 1.5 billion people. After 2013, that is why I started saying strongly and loudly, "This is about the other six billion." That is what financial inclusion means.

Our regulatory system is actively excluding people from finance. We have reached a point where access to basic financial services has become a privilege. The average person must do a dance to prove themselves worthy in front of a banker, filling in reams of paperwork and application forms, to be granted the privilege of financial services. We are even condemning cash: the ultimate peer-to-peer, anonymous, fungible mechanism that has provided basic financial services to everyone for millenia.

The "Fatal Flaw" of Cash

Cash has a fatal flaw, which is not that it is anonymous — that is its greatest feature. It is not that it can be used by criminals, because the real criminals get a banking license and defraud people by the millions. It is available to everyone without vetting. Cash is an open, transparent, verifiable, transportable, peer-to-peer transactional system.

But its greatest weakness is that it is constrained by geography and locality. It doesn't have enough range and scale.

Now we have a new form of digital cash, which is also open, transparent, verifiable, transportable and a peer-to-peer transactional system. But this one is also borderless, neutral, unforgeable, censorship resistant, and can be used even when your government doesn't want you to use it. It does not require privilege or identity. It can be used by anyone, anywhere in the world, by simply downloading the software on whatever computing device you have access to. That is the real revolution here.

In the wealthy nations, we have our privileged little discussions about whether we should regulate cryptocurrencies, how much we should regulate cryptocurrencies, and who should regulate cryptocurrencies but… *Fuck that!* Cryptocurrencies are about providing universal access to basic finance, to anyone who needs it, anywhere in the world, whether we like them or not.

What will people do with universal basic finance? They will do what they have done for millenia with cash. They will build a future for their children.

The Politics of Fear

We are paralyzed with fear because of a few bad actors, blind to the fact that worst actors have state privilege and endorsements, they're hand-in-hand with intelligence agencies, inside the mechanisms of surveillance capitalism. They fund dictators and drug lords all around the world with our tax money, to the tune of trillions of dollars.

The real terrorism and drug financing doesn't happen in petty cash or cryptocurrency; it happens through millions of barrels of oil and U.S. dollar wire transfers, by banks who get caught again and again. They will pay a fine that is worth a fraction of their profit and ignore the tens of thousands of deaths they have contributed to. Not a single person goes to jail.

Some people still have the audacity to say that we must end cash in order to stop crime. How magnificently self-righteous. In the United States, about 18% of the population does not have access to banking services. That is almost 60 million people.

Once, when I recited this fact at a banking conference, a banking regulator in the back raised their hand and asked, "Why should we give bank accounts to illegals?"

That is a chilling question to ask, but let me translate it to you in words that will have more of an impact: "*Those people* don't deserve the privilege of financial inclusion."

When your neighbor says, "*Those people* don't belong in our neighborhood," it might freak you out. You suddenly realize that you are living next to a bigot. But when this banking regulator asked, "Why should we give bank accounts to illegals," I calmly responded, "You shouldn't. We will." (Also, human beings aren't illegal or "illegals.")

The Face of the Unbanked

At the last conference I attended, after I gave my speech decrying the lack of security and financial inclusion, a young man in his 20s came up to me and said, "This really spoke to my personal story." He had been living in western, developed countries for the past fifteen years, and has not been able to open a bank account.

"Every time I write my name and place of birth in the application, the process has already ended. I was born in Iran. I didn't choose that. I haven't done anything wrong. I have a job and I pay my taxes. All I want is to deposit my paycheck and buy groceries. For fifteen years, I've been unable to do that."

This is the face of the unbanked.

They are walking the streets around you, in this city of privilege, the independent district of London, bought and paid for by banking corporations. This enclave is the Vatican of capitalism, a city within a city. Invisible people such as janitors and service professionals making your sandwiches, who don't have a bank account. Maybe they accept checks or other forms of payment they can't deposit. They have to convert these forms of payment into cash, that they must carry or hide. Their loans are through payday loan services at exorbitant interest rates. They are charged 10-30% to send money home to their loved ones and support a basic subsistence lifestyle.

Don't imagine the great masses in Africa, South America, or southeast Asia; of course many of them are unbanked. But the unbanked are also right here. They are your neighbors. They are forced to live in that position so we can continue believing in the illusion that safety comes from totalitarian surveillance.

Moral Bankruptcy

This very conference is being sponsored by a company that is spreading around millions of dollars worth of marketing for surveillance tools. They are promoting and advancing the state-of-the-art. These surveillance companies share and sell your data to other companies, which further process that data to intelligence agencies. This lovely trickle-down surveillance may eventually reach some regime that enjoys cutting up the bodies of journalists with hacksaws.

Don't fool yourself: it is not possible to separate your position within a company like that from the moral implications of your actions.

When you are hiring people, look at the companies they have worked for. When you see a surveillance company which actively sells our data to the highest bidder, know that the candidate has declared moral bankruptcy (just like when you see military-industrial complex companies like General Dynamics, Raytheon, and Lockheed Martin listed). My view is that if you declare moral bankruptcy, you should have to spend at least seven years struggling to find a job and being interrogated about your ethics. These companies should not be resume builders, they should be resume killers.

Former founders and employees of these organizations should struggle for seven years, just like people are forced to spend seven years trying to prove to a banker that they deserve the privilege of banking after filing for financial bankruptcy.

Moral Choices

We have some deep moral choices to make. We stand at a crossroads right now. World governments are trying to abolish cash, the very last lifeline that remains for billions of people. They are trying to implement total financial surveillance, excluding all who aren't deemed worthy. It is not that these people are unworthy because they don't work; they work harder than all of us. It is not because they don't deserve better. It is because of where they were born, the documentation or literacy they don't have, and how they look.

In Saudi Arabia, women are often restricted from owning property and bank accounts. This is the case in half a dozen countries around the world. We look at that and say, "Shame on them. That is immoral. That is disgusting." Then we turn around and do the same thing to immigrants in this country.

I am part British, part American. That means the moment I arrive in dozens of countries around the world, I need to apologize. I know in my heart that every time I pay taxes, I am killing thousands of people by proxy and it makes me sick. But I still pay, because I am also helping people receiving assistance from social welfare programs.

Surveillance Doesn't Stop Crime

When we make these moral choices, we need to understand that surveillance never stopped crime. Surveillance is the license that gives control to people at the top of the system. They will commit crimes, the worst of crimes. I know Britain doesn't use the metric system, so "mega-" is the prefix we use for millions. For example, a mega-crime is where you fraudulently foreclose a million homes, leaving people homeless and hopeless, and don't go to jail.

We perform surveillance and analytics to catch petty drug dealers selling pot for bitcoin, but who is surveilling the actions of Lockheed Martin? Or the money laundering banks? Nobody. Do you know why none of them will ever go to jail? The regulators are completely captured. This is a system of controlling all finance from above, with levers of power over the lives of millions and billions of people, cutting off entire countries because they're under sanction. They are not privileged enough, they are not "people" enough to gain financial services.

Guess what kind of people are attracted to systems like these? If you build levers of power that can be manipulated, the very worst sociopaths in our society are attracted, like flies to shit. They will grab hold of those levers of power and destroy your freedoms as quickly as they can. And one bad election could be the last election. If you don't believe me, look at what has happened in Turkey, Russia, and Venezuela.

The Other Six Billion

Let me end on a positive note, because you are probably a bit freaked out by all of this. You should be. This is serious stuff.

Open, public, borderless, transparent, neutral, censorship resistant, and private cryptocurrencies exist. They will not be regulated; they cannot be regulated. Not by committees, only by mathematics and algorithms. They provide certainty, reputation management, and programmable consumer protection. They provide access without identity.

Eventually, they will give billions of people not just a bank account in their pocket, but a bank. They will democratize the functions of banking, as applications that anyone can access without vetting. People are pre-vetted by simply agreeing to download software which follows the rules of consensus. That is the only vetting required in these systems.

"But we shouldn't allow that!" We did. "But we can't have people making anonymous transactions!" They will. "But we must regulate this!" You can't. And you won't.

Six billion people need this. You have neither the moral authority nor the practical capability to stand in their way.

You can't stand in the way of what will be the greatest revolution in financial services in three centuries. Universal access to basic finance.

Thank you.

Measuring Success: Price or Principle

The original video presentation of this talk was recorded as part of Andreas' *The Internet of Money Tour 2019.* This specific event was hosted by the Dublin Bitcoin Meetup and University College Dublin in Dublin, Ireland; May 2018. Video Link: https://aantonop.io/MeasuringSuccess

To the Moon and Back Again

The topic I want to talk about today is how we measure success. How we measure success in this space says a lot about what our individual goals are. But it also says a lot about how our industry, our ecosystem, our environment is changing over time.

I ask people quite often, "How would you measure success in this space?" Whether we're talking about Bitcoin or open public blockchains and other cryptocurrencies in general, I ask: "What does it mean to be successful? When do we know that we are winning or have won this battle? When do we know that this technology has arrived?" Their answers say a lot about the person I'm talking with. It's a highly personal answer. The silly answer is "when the price goes to the moon!" But that's not a very good measure of success, because that's not what we should be aiming for.

But then again, that's why a lot of people get involved in these technologies. A lot of people get involved at first because they anticipate, or have heard, that this is a fantastic get-rich-quick scheme. Then they discover over the next harrowing weeks — or sometimes just days — that it can also be a fantastic get-poor-quick scheme. As they branch out they get into obscure altcoins they just recently heard of, trade based on panic, try to cut their losses, and blow all of their investment away. If you got into this space to get rich, you may succeed, but you probably won't. That's not a very good motivation.

Building Community

Fortunately, if you have a strong local community, what happens when the price goes shooting up across the cryptocurrency space? A lot of new people start showing up to the meetups with a little sparkle in their eyes. Yeah, you can tell! They're "very excited about this technology." *No, they're not!* They're very excited about the possibility of making some money. As soon as the price turns (which happens on average just after it climbs to the highpoint), most of them disappear.

I've watched these cycles since 2012. The very first Bitcoin meetup I attended was the Napa Valley Bitcoin Meetup. Only one other person showed up, Adam B. Levine, and we ate steak together. Since that meeting, Adam and I have recorded more than 380 episodes of the *Let's Talk Bitcoin* podcast together with Dr. Stephanie Murphy and, more recently, Jonathan Mohan. It's the longest running podcast in the Bitcoin space. But the first time we met, it was just two Bitcoin nerds at a meetup.

Fast-forward to about a year later, and that same meetup had fifty people showing up on a weekly basis. Then about a year after that, there were only five people. If you follow these trends, you'll notice that interest in our industry ebbs and flows like the price.

In order to build community, education is key. Teach people why you are interested in the technology. If you can educate people about the technology, even if they initially joined the community for all of the wrong reasons, they're likely to stay.

Not In It For The Money

If you got into this space between October and December 2017 to get rich and invest money, and you're still here, clearly you're not here for the money. You've weathered the storm. We're on the other side of that mountain now; things are looking pretty grim comparatively. If you're still here, that means you have another motivation. That's great, because now you can start talking to the people around you, in your community, about why you are still interested in this technology and what you think it will do.

For me, the important characteristics of open public blockchains have nothing to do with money. They have a lot to do with decentralizing trust; it's about creating open environments that are borderless, global, and can create opportunities for people to engage in commerce without restrictions. To me, it's about changing the architecture of one of the fundamental technologies we have in society — money.

That is what drives me. I have this wild idea that this technology can change the world. I can see a world where access to this technology changes people's lives — especially in places where there is very little access to financial services, to fair and open systems, or the ability to record the truth. I can see a world where we can transact without trust, kick out intermediaries from every commercial transaction, and get rid of organised criminals who happen to have a banking license and are robbing people blind.

Of course, this is not as much of a problem in Ireland, but it certainly is a problem in the vast majority of the world. To me, those things are important. I measure success a bit differently.

The Conflict of Principles with Mainstream Adoption

When I ask people, "how do you measure success with this technology," the most common answer I receive is "mainstream adoption." By mainstream adoption, they mean most people around them are using the technology and/ or they can use it to buy something from a local store. That's their measure of success and it's a very common measure of success. The vision includes walking into their local store for a breakfast sandwich and not having to ask, "Do you take bitcoin / ether / litecoin / monero?" They obviously do. That's how most people think about success in this industry. This would mean that alongside Visa, Mastercard, cash, euros, and dollars, you could pay in your local shop with one of these weird cryptocurrencies and, most importantly, it would no longer be weird. You would no longer be the weirdo who keeps asking, "Do you take bitcoin?" Been there, done that!

If you ask a few follow-up questions, you'll learn of other measures of success, including whether or not the system maintains its fundamental principles. One of the core principles is that these systems should lead to societal change. People should use cryptocurrencies to free themselves from an inflexible banking system, that we are able to "bank the un-banked" or "de-bank all of us," as you've probably heard me say. These principles are also about introducing more fairness into commerce, giving less power to corporations and more power to individuals.

These are more idealistic goals for success. If you stop for a moment and think about it, you realize those two goals, mainstream adoption and maintaining the principles, are fundamentally at odds.

If the measure of success is mainstream adoption, then maintaining the principles that made us interested in this technology doesn't actually happen. Mainstream adoption means adoption by people who don't care about these principles, the vast majority of people around you. How many people in here care about privacy enough to sacrifice some convenience on a daily basis? How many of the people you know use the same password on every website? How many people here would never share their private information on Facebook? How many people do you know, who think Facebook is the internet and barely leave that space? And vote based on what they see there?

The problem is that mainstream adoption dilutes principles. The mainstream doesn't share your principles, it doesn't share your motivations. You're not the mainstream, you're the weirdos who are into Bitcoin and cryptocurrencies. That's okay. This isn't a mainstream thing and it's important that we recognise that, when we have principles we really care about, we can still affect change in the world even while those principles are being diluted around us.

A Short History of Linux

I want to talk about what success looks like from my perspective, having seen a couple of disruptive technologies in the past that emerged and then got absorbed into mainstream use. I think it's important to see that the measure of success isn't necessarily what you think it is. It is not as obvious as it might seem.

Let me start by asking a question: how many of you here use the Linux operating system? Alright. For those of you who didn't raise your hands… all of you actually use the Linux operating system every single day! It is used in your phones, vacuum cleaners, cars, elevators, and every single web server you touch. It is in the little robots you bought for your kids. It is in your lawnmower. It is in every Android phone. It is even in Windows now.

But that's not how it started. The Linux operating system was started in 1991, by a Finnish student by the name of Linus Torvalds, who had an unconventional idea. At the time, he was too poor to afford a license for one of the commercial Unix-like operating systems that were made by companies like IBM, AT&T, and Sun Microsystems, which sold to other power corporations for thousands of dollars in licensing fees per year. That's how the business of operating systems worked at the time.

But this Finnish student had an idea. He thought, *What if I write my own operating system?* At this point, you have to realize how ridiculous that idea was, on so many levels. The Unix operating system that AT&T created in the 1960s under Bell Labs, then built up by these giant corporations, is the operating system that runs the space program and the mainframes of all the banks. This is serious, heavy-duty, commercial operating system software. Yet this young man said, "Let me write my own."

Most of the people around him treated him exactly as you would your cousin who suddenly says, "I'm going to build my own rocket and colonize Mars on my own!" Everyone says, "Yeah? Okay…" And yet he did it anyway.

Three or four years later, I downloaded an alpha (pre-beta) version of that operating system from his university file server, from his home directory, onto two hundred floppy disks, and installed it on my own personal computer. It barely worked but I was elated. I, as a student, had a Unix operating system on a personal computer that I could control. The same thing that they had at the university and just as powerful.

He had organized a group of programmers and built it. But what is the point of an operating system that is completely open, free for anyone to use and innovate on, for systems as small as embedded microcontrollers or as large as the biggest supercomputers on the planet? They would say that success would be if all of the corporations used it; success would be if we put all of those other operating system companies out of business. Success would be if nobody paid for an operating system like that again.

Reality vs. Expectation

On those measures, ironically, Linux succeeded in all of those things! AT&T no longer makes operating systems, IBM no longer makes operating systems, even Microsoft really no longer makes working operating systems. And now they support Linux, their greatest foe. Linux now runs everything from the smallest Raspberry Pi computer that you can buy for $30 and use to run your sprinkler system in your garden, all the way to every single one of the world's top 100 supercomputers. They all run Linux. Linux is everywhere.

And yet, if you thought mainstream adoption meant that your mom or uncle uses Linux (and knows they're using Linux)… in that measure, it failed. Nobody knows they're using it. It is not branded. Practically nobody uses it on their desktop, apart from a few weirdos: me and others in the audience. Who uses Linux on their desktop? Okay. Yeah. You can see the correlation, right? That's how they get you. It is a gateway drug. You start with Linux on the desktop and eventually you're in an amphitheatre full of cryptocurrency weirdos. It's a slippery slope. *Audience laughs.*

The measure of success is not mainstream adoption. It's not mainstream adoption in the way that you think it is, where everybody knows this is part of their life. It is a much more subtle measure of success.

Linux gave everyone the choice to run an operating system that's extremely powerful; people have the freedom to run it without even knowing that they're running it because it's in their thermostat. But having a free and open source operating system also means that anyone can build a thermostat and start a company that builds thermostats while using an extremely powerful, multi-threaded, robust operating system that has millions of different drivers for different pieces of hardware.

Eventually, every piece of hardware on the planet can be used with this operating system. It is open and everybody is innovating around it. It breaks the monopoly of the big companies and gives that freedom of choice to everyone. It's become mainstream to the point where people no longer know they're using it.

The Success of the Internet

I'll go a bit further back and talk about what it means to measure the success of the internet. Most of the people in this room are too young to remember a time before the internet. I was there; I not only remember it but I grew up in a country where we didn't have computers in my school.

I bought my own computer at 10.5 years old. Well, my mum bought me my own computer when I was 10.5 years old (thank you, Mum). Later, I joined the internet surreptitiously through an account that legally speaking I didn't own, because it was a local university account. At the time I was 14 years old. Details aside, statute of limitations and all that… I got on the internet and it opened this whole world for me.

I suddenly realized that if you got computers to *talk* to each other and they could collaborate using open protocols, this incredible flow of information could start happening. I started telling everyone around me that the internet will change our lives, and nobody believed me.

If you had asked me then what the measure of success was for the internet, I would say, "Everybody uses it. But not just that, it's that we break the back of monopoly publishers like the New York Times, the London Times, the empires of broadcasting. We alter the flow of information from governments to citizens, especially despotic dictatorial regimes that censor their residents. Success is giving access to information to people who had never had it before. Maybe one day, a farmer in Vietnam with a mobile device will be able to read an article written by a German student about the latest advances in agriculture." I could imagine all of these scenarios.

What if we changed the measure of success? What if we defined success as having a very powerful, decentralized network that gave us all access to information? By that measure, the internet has failed. A couple billion people only know the internet as a closed, curated garden called Facebook that gives them carefully filtered information, managed by AI algorithms, to reinforce their existing beliefs and tweak their dopamine receptors so they will buy more plastic shit. That's clearly not the cypherpunk vision of the future that we had hoped for.

At the same time, the internet is highly centralized around a few very important choke points, on to which an entire surveillance infrastructure has been imposed. All of that information is sucked up, processed in vast amounts, and becomes a panopticon. It sounds like a dystopian nightmare. By that measure of success, the internet has failed. It has failed to deliver freedom.

What is it delivering? It's delivering a new set of media moguls to replace the old set, without changing the architecture. I didn't want to switch out Murdoch for Zuckerberg. That doesn't really solve the problem. The goal is: changing the architecture of access to information.

If you look at that, you might think that the internet has failed. But it hasn't, because it is not just made of Facebook. The internet is also mesh networks, relay networks, the dark web, peer-to-peer networks, and Bitcoin! The internet is also wireless communications sent into North Korea, WikiLeaks, whistleblowers, citizen journalists and bloggers who challenge governments by revealing information that those in power don't want revealed. We get to choose which internet we use. A lot of the people in this room are choosing to use the other internet; the free, decentralized, and open internet.

If you look at the big picture, you might say that we failed. If you look more closely, you'll notice that there's an engine of freedom and choice there. It is still capable of birthing these incredible innovations that are unexpected, radically disruptive, and unstoppable, like Bitcoin. It's still able to do that.

So is the internet free, open, and decentralized, or is it not? It's both. It depends which part you're talking about. It has achieved all of its goals, even while a big chunk of the population didn't adopt those principles and simply replaced the old moguls with new moguls in order to get heavily filtered bullshit delivered to them, like a drip feed, through the television.

Nothing changed for some. Everything changed for some.

Corporate Coins

People ask me if I think that big corporations or governments are going to start their own cryptocurrencies, and if they could beat open public blockchains like Bitcoin and Ethereum by replacing them with closed private blockchains. That's basically the same question about how you measure success. What does it mean to go mainstream? What does it mean to beat the open public blockchains at this game?

Let's say that Facebook releases their own coin: FaceCoin. That sounds terrible. Anyway, they release their own coin. You look at it and ask the five basic questions: Is it open? Is it neutral? Is it borderless? Is it decentralized? Is it censorship-resistant?

The answer is no, no, no, no, and no! It is closed, bordered / controlled by jurisdiction, not neutral, absolutely centralized, and censored because it must be. Therefore, it fulfills none of the criteria of an open public blockchain that we care about. It doesn't fulfill any of the principles that we care about.

Maybe the Irish government, through the central bank, releases ÉireCoin. Is it open, borderless, neutral, censorship-resistant, or decentralized? No, no, no, no, and no! It is what we call a central bank digital currency, which is: new suit, same shit!

How do you deal with these phenomena? If you see mainstream adoption as a measure of success, what do you think will be more popular: the free, open, neutral, borderless, decentralized Bitcoin or a closed centralized FaceCoin. In Bitcoin, there's no customer service to call. No I'm sorry — this is a free, decentralized future. Your keys, your coins, and no customer service. Nothing is reversible. With great freedom comes great responsibility.

Isn't that what you wanted? "No, that's not what we wanted. What we wanted was FaceCoin, where every time you do a hundred transactions, you get a little purple star. If you collect five purple stars, you get a free Frappuccino at Starbucks! All I have to do is sell my soul and all of my privacy, and make Zuckerberg the king of the universe." That doesn't seem like the original cypherpunk plan.

If the measure of success is going mainstream, realize that a whole bunch of the mainstream is far more interested in using the loyalty reward points of ÉireCoin, FaceCoin, or some other crap coin that is centralized and controlled. They will not follow your principles.

That means, in many cases, the local chippy won't take your bitcoin even while they do take FaceCoin, AppleCoin, or whatever other corporate concoctions are created.

We have to understand that there will be closed, centralized systems. Those systems will appear faster and cheaper. We don't beat PayPal or Visa, we don't change the banking system, by doing what they do, becoming them but only "weirder." We have to realize that in countries like Ireland where the banking system and payment networks mostly work, the need for a decentralized currency like this isn't quite there. You don't need bitcoin, yet.

Who Needs Bitcoin?

Ask a Venezuelan if they need bitcoin; the answer is yes. Someone from Argentina, Brazil, Ukraine, Greece, Cyprus… they need it. People who live under despotic governments and dictatorships, people who are fighting revolutions, people who are dealing with currency controls and corrupt banks, people who can't trade internationally. People who do not have sufficient documentation to open a bank account, people trying to transmit money to their relatives across borders in conflict areas… they need it. They need something that is free, open, borderless, and censorship-resistant. They need that for smart contracts, privacy, and currency itself.

You can buy a fish and chips with the euro. You don't need to use bitcoin to do that. If mainstream adoption means adapting by massively diluting the principles, then we lose the game. That is not a measure of success, that is a measure of failure.

Keep the Principles

The measure of success to me is keeping the principles — remaining free, open, decentralized, neutral, and censorship-resistant — while becoming available to the people who need it around the world. That's my measure of success.

That measure of success is very different from what we often see in our industry. As you may have noticed, over the last couple of years, a lot of new money and suits have shown up in the cryptocurrency space. They may talk the talk, but they don't want to change the architecture of the financial system. They don't want to break the monopolies, crush the cartels, break open access to financial systems, or give economic inclusion to as many people as possible. *They simply want to replace the old layer of the top 1% with themselves.* They think, *The architecture is fine if I'm on top.* They likely do not share your measure of success.

Market Capitalization is a Terrible Metric

Another (very pernicious) measure of success you commonly see in our space is market capitalization. How many people have heard or seen that term in relation to bitcoin, ether, or other cryptocurrencies? How many people have heard of the Dominance Index? The Dominance Index is a percentage of the total market capitalization of cryptocurrencies owned by bitcoin.

Here's why this is not a good metric and why we shouldn't look at it for any of the cryptocurrencies. Market capitalization tells you which is the richest cryptocurrency. I can guarantee you that there will be cryptocurrencies richer, bigger, more broadly accepted than bitcoin. It is very easy to do that, all you have to do is sacrifice the principles. You can make something that is cheap, fast, centralized, controlled, and censored. Then you can pump money into it and make it mainstream. FaceCoin will be bigger than bitcoin. FedCoin will be bigger than bitcoin. Hell, Ripple may be bigger than bitcoin sometime soon. Ultimately this is about changing the architecture of finance, at least to me.

What do the banks have that we don't? Money! What's the worst way to measure success in our industry? Who has the biggest amount of money. Well, we've already lost that game to the banks, they have all of it. They print it from nothing and control the creation process. Their entire industry is rent-seeking. Of course they have money!

What they don't have is creativity, innovation, morality, sustainability, and a plan for how to get the hell out of quantitative easing. They don't have any of those things, but they have plenty of money. If you wanted to really screw with a nascent, disruptive industry, what better way to utterly confuse everyone than to persuade them that the measure of success is the fuel of the status-quo? "We will measure this new, disruptive industry by the metric that we succeed at already: money!"

Being the biggest cryptocurrency is worthless, if you must sacrifice being the free cryptocurrency. If you sacrifice liberty, decentralization, and neutrality to become the biggest, all you've done is recreated the status-quo but replaced the people at the top. To me, that is a measure of failure.

The Measure of Success is Liberty

Bitcoin is not going to be the biggest. Especially because of how difficult it is to change this system — which is a great feature, because everyone is trying to change it right now — and remove these pesky freedom principles.

What I hope isn't that we, the bitcoin community, are the biggest, but that we have the most free, inclusive, open system of commerce on the planet. If that means we're not going to be the biggest, I will take that! If you want to win, if you care about the principles, if you're still here after the price drops, and you really want to see this technology succeed, the most important thing you have to do is to have a clear perspective on what the measure of success is.

The measure of success is liberty.

Thank you!

Libre Not Libra: Facebook's Blockchain Project

The original video presentation of this talk was recorded as part of Andreas' *The Internet of Money Tour 2019*. This specific event was hosted by the Scottish Blockchain Meetup in Edinburgh, Scotland; June 2019. Video Link: https://aantonop.io/LibreNotLibra

The Burning Question

I think you are all probably thinking the same thing. You have a burning question. I felt like I wouldn't be able to do the rest of my speaking tour without addressing this burning question. I was bombarded on Twitter today with the same question: "Have you tasted haggis?"

The answer is, "No, I'm too scared." I made the mistake of reading about how it's made before tasting it. I've been told that you should do it the other way around, because then it is a lot less scary. I'm trying to build up the courage. I have been told that the best way to eat it is in a burger. I don't know if that is actually true. No? Okay. There is a big disagreement in the room.

On the count of three, all those in favor of haggis burger, raise your hand. Nobody? Okay. Haggis for breakfast? *Audience cheers.* Are there other formulations I should try? *Audience member calls out "Haggis on toast!"* Haggis on toast is what I should try then. How about a corporate-sponsored haggis that is pretending to be an open haggis? And was launched this morning? *Everyone laughs.*

Let's talk about the elephant in the room: Libra. You've probably heard that this morning Facebook announced their own cryptocurrency, Libra. For many people the idea of Facebook getting into cryptocurrency is scary.

Whenever the mainstream news outlets report that the price of bitcoin has crashed, I receive calls from friends and family, asking if I am okay. "Are you okay? Is everything okay?" Today, I actually got a call from a friend's mother. She asked me if I'm okay and the price has not even dropped! Just the fact that Facebook launched a cryptocurrency led to the "Are you okay?

Are you holding up?" question. "Do we need to airlift you out of Europe?" Don't worry everyone, I am okay. We're all okay.

The Libra Whitepaper

Some years ago I talked about Facebook launching their own coin. I expected that one day we would see this happen. And today is the day; it is now happening. But what exactly happened?

This morning, Facebook released a whitepaper. Not a cryptocurrency. Not a network. Not a project. Not even an application. Just a whitepaper. Everybody is freaking out because they wrote a whitepaper. But there is a long road between a whitepaper and a production network available to two billion users, wrapped in a candy-colored Farmville interface.

When they released the whitepaper, some people became really excited. How many of you read the whitepaper? Excellent, quite a few. I'll be honest with you, I did a brief skim. It has been a busy day. I received a bunch of calls from journalists who wanted to talk about it. I am not ready to talk about it from a technology perspective; I need more time to study it. So instead of talking about what Libra is planning to implement, I want to talk about what has changed.

Everything changed this morning.

Whether or not Facebook is able to get Libra into production, this changes everything. The mere fact that this whitepaper was published has now set the bar. Facebook dropped the gauntlet. Silicon Valley is coming for banking in a big way. We predicted that this would happen. A lot of people thought it would be Amazon first. But turns out, it is Facebook - which is much worse than anyone had imagined.

The whitepaper is a collaboration between about twenty companies. I have a feeling that they created an incubator / sandbox innovation lab, gathered thirty to forty bright people, locked them in a room, and slid pizzas under the door until the whitepaper came out. Upon first glance, the whitepaper is actually very impressive, in terms of the technology vision.

These people are very serious. They seem well-informed about what we are doing in the cryptocurrency and blockchain space. They cherry-picked some features of the best cryptocurrencies, the state-of-the-art technology, and then they plan to advance it a bit. They synthesized it into something that sounds quite impressive from a technology perspective.

Libra has taken ideas from Ethereum, like a virtual machine for execution of smart contracts and gas. A Merkle state tree that can be added to Merkle Mountain Ranges, or the Ethereum state tree. An embedded or intrinsic digital currency. A proof-of-authority, federated network of validators, similar to Ripple or EOS, things that are kind of blockchains but not quite. Their consensus algorithm is not exactly new. It is a Byzantine fault tolerant consensus algorithm, which is not proof-of-work, but they say they want to move it to proof-of-stake. There is some very interesting stuff in the whitepaper. They mashed these components together and created something that is impressive from a technology perspective.

But it is impressive because of who did it, not because of what was actually done. If I had released that whitepaper with a bunch of collaborators, everybody would have shrugged it off. "Okay, there's another blockchain..." But when a company with two billion users does that, people understand that this could have a big impact. Now we will see whether this idea survives its first contact with Facebook's corporate managers.

Will The Vision Survive Deployment?

At the moment, this is an incubated project. It is idealistic. It is rather aggressive in its vision. It is focused on being decentralized, a bit now and even more in the future. Permissioned now, permissionless in the future. Proof-of-authority now, proof-of-stake in the future. A very progressive, aggressive vision.

But that vision will run straight into a bunch of MBAs and lawyers at Facebook headquarters. It will be really interesting to see how much of this vision, if any, survives into deployment. That will determine what happens next. If it survives into deployment, it could become very successful and a huge moneymaker. Then MBAs will become very excited.

Some things in the whitepaper are quite surprising. For example, the use of an association to segregate it from Facebook, and a promise to not use the profile information on your Facebook account.

Do you have a personal Facebook account? I sure as hell don't. Will they use that in collaboration with the currency? That would be a no-no, right?

At the moment, it says that information will not be shared and used for surveillance. It will not be used for any of these-

A cell phone notification interrupts the talk. Oh, one second. Sorry. *Andreas looks at his phone and begins to read aloud in a lawyerly voice.*

"We are sending you this very important email to notify you about changes to our Terms & Conditions. Please read the following 600 pages of gibberish to understand how we've completely removed due process and your privacy. Thank you very much! -The Facebook Team."

So that email just came to me from the future. Or rather, I expect an email like that to be sent sometime in the future.

Those progressive promises will change the moment this becomes successful. If you think that I'm kidding, look at what happened to WhatsApp. The founders of that company started with the same kind of idealistic vision. But after the Facebook acquisition, the founders ended up leaving in protest, forgoing hundreds of millions of dollars in stock options. **Do not use WhatsApp if you are a dissident, an activist, or a political operative.** If your communication's confidentiality will make the difference between surviving or not, if you are one of the millions of people marching in Hong Kong this week, don't use WhatsApp.

Will something similar happen with Libra and its idealistic vision? I'm a bit of a cynic. I think that large corporations have a tendency to swallow innovation, rip out the disruptive parts, and spit out something safely neutered. Something that is profit-making, exploiting users whenever necessary, because they have to make money for their shareholders. But we will see. Maybe this time it will be different.

From a technical perspective, a whitepaper outlining a progressive, aggressive vision of a Facebook-driven cryptocurrency was published today. That's all.

The Three-Body Problem

But the technical vision in the whitepaper isn't why this changes everything. It changes everything because now there's a three-body problem. Before this announcement, the industry was viewed mostly as the interaction between two major forces: on one side, we have nation-state fiat money, as we derisively call it in the crypto space; on the other side, we have the people's money, open and borderless cryptocurrency for everyone to use.

These two forces are orbiting and exerting pressure on each other. Right now, cryptocurrencies are a bunch of little asteroids. Fiat is a big planet full of very successful life forms, who are looking up at the sky and wondering, "What is that shiny thing? It seems to be getting bigger." You know, the experience of the dinosaurs. "Don't worry, it's pretty. Look at how nice the sunset looks!" "Oh, it keeps getting bigger…"

Solving the two-body problem from a political perspective, trying to figure out what happens when nation-states and open cryptocurrencies collide, is difficult enough. We don't know the answer because nations are positioning themselves in different ways. Some are freaked out and ban it outright. China has reportedly attempted to ban it numerous times so far. All ineffectively. India has banned it, kind of, twice. Ecuador was one of the first to ban it completely.

Yet in many advanced nations, cryptocurrencies have actually been thriving. In what we call free societies, the idea of banning private currency is constitutionally problematic. Both the United States' Constitution and the United Kingdom's constitution protect freedom-

Oh, wait. You don't have a constitution… *Andreas smiles and the audience laughs.*

The Magna Carta, let's say, protects freedom of speech. And free speech is cherished in free societies. Money is a form of political speech. It is not so easy to just ban cryptocurrencies, at least in free societies.

Corporate Currencies

But there was a lot of tension this morning, with a big discussion on Twitter that I reluctantly got involved in. It was about whether Facebook's Libra is a cryptocurrency or not.

Let's take a quick poll. All those who say that it is a cryptocurrency, raise your hand. *About 30 people sheepishly raise a hand.* All those who say it is not, raise your hand. *About 25 people more boldly raise a hand.* All those who haven't decided yet, raise your hand. *Almost everyone raises their hands, the audience laughs.*

Yes, I know the poll doesn't make sense.

It doesn't make sense because Facebook's Libra is new. It is a corporate digital currency. We haven't seen corporate currencies since the opium wars, medieval feudalism, and the Medici. How fitting that with the dawn of corporate neo-feudalism, one of the leading corporate states, the supra-nation of Facebook, is launching its own currency.

Things will become very interesting, for a number of reasons. We now have a three-point stand-off. It is now money of the corporations, money of the people, and the money of government.

All three will exist. None of them are going away soon. In fact, more will join. The doors have been opened. Facebook is the first of the FANGs; the rest are baring their fangs and ready to go. FANGs, if you don't know, stands for Facebook-Amazon-Netflix-Google... and the billion-dollar tech companies of Silicon Valley. There is also Twitter, Uber, and Airbnb but they don't fit nicely into that acronym.

Silicon Valley is Coming for Banking

Silicon Valley is coming for the banks, in a way that has never happened before. The bankers have been very comfortable until now. In 2014, I spoke to banking executives at a conference in Zurich and I told them, "Listen. Instead of hiring blockchain consultants to show you how to square a circle, undo the disruption, and pretend to do blockchain, you should hire a former executive from the music industry. Ask them what it felt like when the internet came for their industry. When did you realize you couldn't do anything about it? How did it feel when you started losing to Apple? What would you have done differently?"

Guess what? The banks had more than ten years to figure this shit out. They had more than ten years to figure out how they would handle digital currencies. The music industry should have made a deal with Napster; instead, they fought with tooth and nail, and handed the industry to Apple. The banks should have made a deal with bitcoin when it was the cuddly gecko of cryptocurrencies. Facebook is a Triceratops of social media and it is coming for their industry.

It may sound really weird, but the first to be affected by corporate currencies will be retail banks. Not the big bad investment banks who make shady deals to bail out dictators and stuff like that. It's the banks that actually serve customers that will be affected first. Most big investment banks stopped taking checking and savings customers in consumer markets four or five years ago. "You people don't pay enough. You're not worthy of banking." But it will impact the retail banks, the corner branch where you know the banker, or at least you can call them to discuss your overdraft ballooning again. Those retail banks actually serve customers, even the underbanked. They will be hit hard by this new phenomenon, because Facebook not only has two billion users, but they know all their preferences and behavior patterns.

Facebook can drop the cost of banking and wrap it in a candy-colored user interface. Every time you make a purchase with Libra, the application could tickle your dopamine receptors a bit. It will encourage you to do or not do certain things, play with you like a mouse in a psychology experiment, where you can't see the edges of the maze because the walls are too high. This will be very interesting as it plays out.

Central Bankers Beware

To those of us who have been paying attention to the rise of techno neo-feudalism, it is terrifying. Corporate currencies will be effective at disrupting regulation in a way that banks have not been able to. Facebook is now going after central banks. Yes, Libra has a basket of currencies to create some kind of stablecoin thing, but that stablecoin will be stable vis-à-vis your local currency that is hyperinflating.

Imagine that you are the government in India or Argentina, and you want to follow an inflation or devaluation policy, but 10% of your population has moved on to Libra or another corporate currency. With Libra they could put their savings in the hard currency of Facebook. Well, not really a hard currency. It doesn't really have a monetary policy, so they say, but it is harder than the Argentine peso. It is harder than the Turkish lira, the Indian rupee, and more than a hundred currencies around the world. Corporate currencies mean that central banks will lose one of the big levers of power they have over the economy.

What will they do, ban Facebook? They will try. They have been trying to ban Facebook during protests, coup d'états of dictatorships, and revolutions.

They will fail. They will try to regulate Facebook and they'll be facing an army of Wall Street lawyers saying "Let's talk about these regulations."

If you didn't realize it, Facebook is planning to launch consumer and retail level SDRs. Who knows what an SDR is? A few people. The International Monetary Fund (IMF) is a global institution that is not officially controlled by governments. It uses contributions from member states, a basket of currencies, to issue an artificial currency called Special Drawing Rights (SDRs). SDRs are part of the international framework of free-floating exchange rates. The IMF is the lender of last resort for governments. They do so in a very predatory manner. They impose extreme austerity on governments which fall into their clutches, asset-strip their industries, their water plants, railroads, and telecommunications companies.

Well, guess what? Facebook could do that now. If you think about what Libra claims to be, it is actually a Special Drawing Rights pseudo-currency, based on a basket of currencies, that is funded by consumer activity, in the same countries where the government will ask them for a loan or try to curtail their activity. This is very serious stuff. We just went post-national.

The power to control money used to be the exclusive prerogative of states. That has been kicked in the nuts by Bitcoin and threatened with decapitation by Libra this morning. Central bank control over monetary policy ended this morning. Technology companies currently worth a trillion dollars total are taking the ability to mint their own money. They will radically transform their business models, generating more money than you can ever imagine. Shareholders will be thrilled. Soon they will dwarf the GDP of at least one third of the nations on this planet.

When the IMF comes calling, most governments cower in fear. But imagine how much worse it will be when Facebook, Google, or Apple comes calling. Maybe even Twitter can take down a few governments. It is big enough. Why not? Soon, maybe Uber will be dictating not just to taxi drivers, but to the local council and maybe even the cabinet of ministers.

We've entered a new world in which three forces will be competing: money of the people, money of the state, and money of the corporations. We need to make some very careful choices.

I am hopeful for a number of reasons. The corporations will contribute to the technology, whether they want to or not. They will introduce a billion people to the wrong kind of cryptocurrency, just like AOL introduced people to the wrong kind of internet.

The Five Pillars of Open Blockchains

But here is where it gets tricky. At this point, we need to decide how to differentiate based on our principles. I have talked about the fundamental principles I care about in blockchains. Sometimes I call them the five pillars of open blockchains, or the eight criteria. I lose count. It is somewhere between five and eight, but you should always scrutinize a system that is trying to take over the foundational technology of money in your world.

Is it open? What does "open" mean? Is it open for anyone to access and participate without vetting? Can anyone send a transaction without providing identification? Is it? We don't know yet. We will see. The whitepaper claims it is open. We will need to wait and see what the currency actually does.

Is it borderless? I can tell you right now, it will not be borderless. There is only one borderless, global cryptocurrency of any value and meaning today. That is bitcoin. Libra might be as good as the U.S. dollar at being borderless but Libra will not launch in China. Instead they will have their own, launched by WeChat or a subsidiary wholly owned by the People's Republic of China, the central politburo. It will not launch in Russia either. Are they going to give up their monetary sovereignty to a dude from Silicon Valley? It will not launch in a bunch of other places with unbanked people who actually need financial services. It will not be borderless. In fact, quite the opposite.

We have entered the era of Cold War-esque currency wars. An Iron Curtain for currencies will drop, like we have never seen before. We will see a split between East and West in the evolution of state-based and corporate currencies. Of the three, only open cryptocurrencies will go everywhere around the world.

Is it neutral? Libra will probably not be neutral. Neutrality requires that the protocol allows transactions from anyone to anyone, anywhere, for any purpose. A lot of open cryptocurrencies do that. I very much doubt that Libra will do that. The moment they allow that, the subpoenas will start flying. The most important detail for a subpoena is knowing where to serve it, right? That will be easy. They have an office which accepts service of process, so that is where governments will send the subpoenas.

Where do you send the Bitcoin subpoenas? Aha! Send them to 127.0.0.1 (localhost IP address), we will process them immediately. *Audience and Andreas laugh.*

So it will not be neutral.

Will it be censorship resistant? It will not be censorship resistant. Large corporations like that, bound by jurisdictional regulations, are obliged to censor transactions. As an American, you cannot send a transaction to an Iranian, a Venezuelan, or a North Korean. You cannot receive money from a Russian or Chinese citizen without properly vetting who they are, when they were born, where they live, and which companies they own. This happens every time you try to send a wire transfer.

Will it be immutable? Libra will not be immutable. They say in the whitepaper that it will be immutable, but the moment you make a transaction funding some abhorrent and inexcusable activity, subpoenas will start flying and the "immutable" network will be muted pretty damn fast. That is pretty easy to do when you have a consortium of validators and no cost for modifying the history.

Proof-of-work makes it practically impossible, even if 100% of the miners collude and try to change history, without expending the same amount of energy. This means with every day that passes, the energy cost increases. Within a day or two, it is an undue burden. It is almost impossible, even if you could find and coerce all of the miners. They wouldn't be able to do it. It is not "won't," it is "can't." Can't is much better than won't. But Libra will not be immutable.

It might be auditable and transparent. We don't know yet. If it is auditable and transparent, it will not be private. We are probably only a few years from another giant leak, where all of your financial data *belong to us*. If it is stored in the blockchain in a transparent manner and you don't have any privacy controls — you know, the kind that "criminals" use, but at least they are smart about privacy — all of that information will be leaked. All of your purchases will now be visible to your friends, family, ex-partners and enemies.

Financial Privacy is a Human Right

Financial privacy is a human right. Society doesn't work as a panopticon. We have secrets because we're social animals. That gives us the freedom to express our freaky nature. We all differ a bit from the expectations and conformity of society. At least, I hope we do. Because if we don't, what kind of society is that? Must we absolutely conform to the expectations of your pretentious neighbors?

Individuality, expression, freedom is privacy. We don't want our financial records blasted to the world. But that will happen next with Libra. It may be auditable and transparent, but not very private. This is not a blockchain I'm interested in.

More importantly, as I have said many times before, we are standing at a fork in the road. On the one hand, we have government and now corporate surveillance money. On the other, we have free, open, and private peoples' money.

The timetable to cashless societies has accelerated. Cashless societies are nothing to celebrate. They will be without freedom or democracy. They are fragile, without the possibility of an exit plan or release valve. Where one election could be the last. You only need to get it wrong once. Just stay at home and say, "I don't care about politics." A bunch of confused, propagandized people go out and vote for an orange man, Brexit, or some shit like that. You ask, "What the hell happened?"

In a world where you don't have cash, where you don't have free, open money, it is much worse than that. The government, a corporation, or payment processor can decide that you have done something "bad," and cut you off from the system, they can turn off your financial future. They could make sure that you can't even buy food, let alone pay for rent or utilities. If you think this isn't happening, it is happening right now in Hong Kong. It is happening in China with the Sesame credit score system.

If you think that is not coming to a country like yours, study up on European history, like 1918 through 1945. Fascinating shit. We thought the U.K. had learned that lesson. From what I have been seeing lately, nope. They are trying to repeat all of that. I guess sometimes you need to teach the lesson twice.

Differentiating on Principles

What will we do in the crypto space? We will start differentiating. Over the next couple of years, expect a lot of crypto projects to focus on what their principles are because principles are the primary way to differentiate between any of the cryptocurrencies. If you are a crypto project, you must decide what your principles are.

I have been expressing the same consistent principles for the last seven years. The reason is really simple: it takes too much bloody homework to shift between different ones, and remember how to be consistent with what I said before. Consistency is relatively easy because I follow principles I actually believe in.

Some crypto projects recently decided to focus on different principles and tried to change the trajectory of projects we care about. Lately, one of them is all about cheap payments, at the expense of decentralization and privacy. Apparently, to the people involved in it, privacy is only useful for illegals and money launderers who are engaging in wash trading and bucket shops. Ooh, scary! If that is the road you want to go down, the light you see is not the end of the tunnel. Instead it's an oncoming Facebook train that already has the principle-less, privacy-less market staked out. They already have two billion users, lots of money and technology people who will run right over you.

If you haven't differentiated based on your principles — or worse, you don't have any principles — and decided with your recently hired MBA that you are really interested in shareholder return on investment, and the best way to do that means shedding a few of these "silly," "idealistic" principles, then guess what? Once you start shedding principles, now you're competing against Facebook.

What is Facebook, if not the world's most powerful principle shedding machine?

It started with few principles to begin with, and has since developed a mechanism for shedding them faster than you can imagine, with billions of dollars in marketing tickling your dopamine receptors. "Don't worry! The future is candy colored and bright... as long as we are still profitable." They can shed principles faster, with more money, better user interfaces, and a bigger user base than you. They have entire committees of MBAs designed to give up principles at high profitability. They will sacrifice principles and judge their performance metrics by it.

"How many principles did we sacrifice this month?" "Three hundred core principles are no longer present." "Not good enough! I want to see 6% growth in the sacrifice of principles month-on-month." *Audience laughs.*

They have the money and the ruthlessness. They do not give a shit about these messages. If you want to compete against them in that area, they will throw principles at you so fast you will lose count. So if your game is shedding principles to make profit, that is a game you will not win. Facebook will win that game. They will win it over PayPal and JPMorgan Chase. They will sure as hell win it over a little ragtag crypto project that says, "We don't need privacy. We just want to be a fast payment network that collaborates with law enforcement and enables surveillance capitalism." Figure out what your principles are.

If you get into a fight with someone who doesn't hold principles, a corporation, that is not immoral, because that requires having negative morality. They are amoral, which means no moral guidance whatsoever. The absence of any moral compass. Morality doesn't even enter their ROI equation. Morality is not on the spreadsheet.

If you are going to pick a fight with them, differentiate on the thing they can't compete with: align yourself with a project that is truly open, borderless, neutral, censorship resistant, transparent, auditable, private, and immutable. There are a few of those, I think. Privacy currencies will get quite a run for their money. There is a growing need to really focus on privacy, because Facebook won't.

The Rising Dystopia

Things just got really interesting. As a technologist, I am so excited. I have been jumping up and down all day. I can't wait to see how this plays out. Watching technological systems interact with society and change the world has been my lifelong fascination. As these developments roll out, I will see if I can pick up a few clues as to where these things are going. To have that vision has been my life's goal.

While as a technologist, I have been jumping up and down, as a human being, I am horrified that we are opening the door to a future that is truly terrifying and dystopian. We are giving power to some of the most ruthless, unaccountable corporations out there. Not to fight against governments, but in many cases to join them hand-in-hand. They will ensure that while we're exploited by ruthless politicians on one side, we are also exploited by ruthless business people on the other, in an alliance between corporation and state.

That is called fascism, only this isn't your grandpa's fascism. This is a whole neo-feudal environment that we have never seen before. A lot of people will make the mistake of assuming that if it doesn't come in a leather uniform designed by Hugo Boss, with clashing colors, caricature parades, and screaming into megaphones, it is not fascism. Fascism today can come in a slick user interface with beautiful colors, accessible 24/7, through your browser and the most convenient location whether your phone is on or off. It is part of your life. It allows you to share photos with Grandpa, the same one who fought Nazis. It is the ultimate irony.

We need to be very careful about what we do next. This is deadly serious stuff. Society is not ready for this because we've never been here before. While I am fascinated to watch, at the same time, I am deeply troubled. It's not that I think Bitcoin can't compete. I am afraid because I believe a lot of people don't care, won't care (until it's too late). A lot of people will go for the easy, convenient, mindless, repetitive, seductive, hypnotizing rhythm of a Facebook feed, through which they will lose their freedom and their future.

But you're here now, and you do have a choice. You can choose the open, borderless, transparent system. You can choose freedom, privacy, and a future you control.

Thank you.

Publisher's note: The Libra whitepaper was released by the Facebook-owned subsidiary Calibra and Swiss-based Libra Association on June 18th 2019. You can read the text in full here: https://libra.org/en-US/white-paper/

Following months of intense media and government scrutiny, PayPal was the first company to pull out of the Libra Association in early October.

Mastercard, Visa, Stripe, Booking Holdings, eBay, and MercadoPago soon followed suit. Facebook CEO Mark Zuckerberg testified about Libra before the U.S. Congress on October 23rd, 2019 at one point stating that "Facebook will not be part of launching the Libra payment system anywhere in the world until US regulators approve."

Inside Out: Money as a System of Control

The original video presentation of this talk was recorded at the *Advanced Digital Innovation Summit* in Vancouver, Canada; September 2017. Video Link: https://aantonop.io/InsideOut

The Four Functions of Money

The topic of today's talk is an interesting property of money that I want to explore with you. I am calling this talk, "Inside Out: Money as a System of Control."

Who can tell me what the four primary functions of money are? Anybody?

Someone in the audience calls out, "Value exchange?" Medium of exchange, that is one. *Another person, "Store of value?"* Store of value, that is two. Two more. Unit of account, is the third. What is the fourth? It's system-of-control (SoC).

What? I don't remember reading that in economics. System-of-control, as it turns out, has become a primary function of the money we use today. Let's talk about it.

The Bank Secrecy Act

We have had money for tens of thousands of years. It is really hard to tell how far back money goes. But the money we have today is very different from the money we have had in the past; something changed in the last 50 years that has fundamentally altered the course of money, of currency, which is a system for communicating value to other people. You're probably familiar with three of the functions of money: medium of exchange (MoE), unit of account (UoA), and store of value (SoV). Those have been around for millenia.

And then something happened. In 1970, Richard Nixon signed the Bank Secrecy Act (BSA) and turned money into a system of control. A system of control that uses money as a political tool, to control who is able to send or receive it, and who you are able to send money to. Ultimately, it aims for the complete surveillance of all financial transactions worldwide. Complete, total, totalitarian financial surveillance. This change in the policies of the USA, 50 years ago, has gradually percolated to almost every country in the world, to almost every financial service in the world, to almost every bank in the world.

In 1970, Richard Nixon effectively deputized the financial services field, to turn them into a branch of law enforcement. Law enforcement that is beyond borders, beyond jurisdictions, beyond due-process, beyond political democratic control and recourse. A cop can confiscate your money. A judge can sign a warrant to freeze your accounts. A bank can do both without authorisation from anyone and there is nothing you can do about it. This applies world-wide. Now, money as a system of control supersedes all other functions of money.

When money is turned into a tool of control, the other functions start eroding. It is no longer the best medium of exchange, because its function as a medium of exchange is subordinate to its function as a system of law enforcement, a system of control. It is no longer the best store of value, for the same reasons. The system of control corrupts these functions of money, diluting them, superseding them.

The Lagging Financial Revolution

We are now 25 years into the internet revolution. Smartphones, cellphones, dumb phones, and other tools for accessing the internet have propagated out to more than 2.5 billion people who have never had these technologies before. But where is finance? Lagging fifteen to twenty years behind. Financial services have not yet reached 2.5 billion people who are completely unbanked and 4 billion people who are underbanked. Only about 1.5 billion people have the full, privileged, elite form of banking that we enjoy in most western liberal democracies.

Even liberal democracies, there are tiers of access and control. How many people in this room are accredited investors? Ah, what a lovely bunch. That puts you in the 1/10 of the 1/10 of the 1/10 percentile of the world.

There are tiers within the financial system. Some people have better access and recourse, and some people have complete immunity. Some people can commit crimes against millions: robo foreclosures, Libor fraud, rigging the gold markets. And they won't go to jail. Why? Because when money becomes a system of control, financial services companies become deputies in this system of enforcement and control. As deputies, they get some perks. One of the perks is immunity: they never go to jail.

Well, with a few exceptions; there are some fundamental rules that always apply to our society. Bernie Madoff went to jail. He made the mistake of stealing from rich people. Don't do that! Foreclose the homes of 10 million poor people? Create 3.5 million fake accounts in Wells Fargo? No problem. Lose 143 million private records of individuals through a hack at Equifax? How many executives will go to jail? I bet none.

Adding a system-of-control function corrupts the basis of money until it can no longer function as a medium of exchange. It breeds economic exclusion.

The Devil's Bargain

We are now 25 years into the internet era, billions are connected, yet we have not expanded the scope of economic inclusion. Historically, we are actually backtracking. Increasingly, entire countries are being cut off from the world financial system. You don't act in the best interests of the United States of America? You lose your SWIFT code; you are no longer part of the wire transfer network. You will submit to the universal jurisdiction of American courts, like Switzerland had to do, or you lose access to international banking, you lose access to the reserve currency, you lose access to the lifeblood of trade.

This devil's bargain has made financial services unassailable from a point of competition perspective. They are surrounded by a thicket of regulations; these regulations are not about consumer protection, consumers are most certainly not protected. They are, most certainly, about the system of control of money. They are about the policy enforcement, and sometimes politics enforcement, that comes with money. Money does not flow freely.

However, I have some bad news. Those gold bars surrounding and protecting banks from competition are a gilded cage. A cage that keeps them inside a system of regulation, prevents competition from the outside, but also prevents them from acting on innovative ideas in free markets or expanding their businesses, unless they subordinate it to a system of control.

The store-of-value use case no longer works. People cannot store value in a currency that can be confiscated on a whim, frozen by any banker, at any point in time. That is not a stable store-of-value. Countries cannot use it as a currency reserve to buy oil, or as a foreign exchange reserve within the country. Because if you cross the superpowers, they will cut off your access and you will not be able to buy oil. Money cannot be a medium of exchange if you cannot exchange it freely. Gradually, the corruption spreads and spreads.

Outside the Gilded Cage

Now, something new has arrived on the horizon: a system of money that operates on a network. It is first and foremost a medium of exchange, a store of value, and one day (potentially) a unit of account. But it will never become a system of control; it refuses to become a system of control. In fact, its design principles are neutrality, openness, borderless access, censorship resistance.

The banks can't play in that space. They are stuck inside their gilded cage, playing cop for superpowers and only offering financial services to a tiny fraction of the human population. They are sacrificing 4 billion people on the altar of poverty in order to create a nice, fake, bourgeois sense of security among the middle class — by selling them lies. FDIC: *Don't worry, your money is insured.* Right?

The Illusion of Protection

How many people here have FDIC or equivalent insurance on their bank accounts? How many Greeks do you think had insurance on their bank accounts? All of them. What happened to that? Their savings went 'poof!' in one afternoon. Vanished, with a 20% haircut.

Whose insurance is it? Does it insure you or does it insure the banks? What does it insure against? Small failure, not big failures. Big failures are uninsurable.

How many of you have money in banks? None of you have money in banks. I mean, please. You have an account, which is a legal construct that they give you in exchange for giving them your money as an unsecured loan, so that they can finance credit to their customers. Technically you might own the money in the account, but possession is how much of the law? Let's see. What happens if you try to withdraw a large amount of money in cash? Or what happens if you cross the wrong person, go to the wrong protest, associate with the wrong organisation, or vote for the wrong party? Then you too might realize that your legal ownership becomes nothing more than a broken promise.

Sure, maybe that is not happening in Canada. But out of a hundred and ninety-four countries, this model of turning money into a system of control has taken off like wildfire, because it is every dictator's wet dream. It ensures that political dissent can be snuffed at the bank, very effectively. It is one of the most effective systems of control in existence.

The Power of Voice and Exit

Now bankers must face competition from a system which will not do that, cannot be made to do that, will not yield or be co-opted. What is their response? "Bitcoin is a joke." "Cryptocurrencies are outside the system." "Nobody wants to be outside the system." Guess what? There are roughly 7 billion people on our planet. Most of them don't want to be outside the system; they would much rather be inside. But they haven't been invited and they probably won't be. Many of them can't do the things that are necessary to be invited into the system, like produce a valid identification document or change their country of birth.

There is an entire generation that has discovered the two vital forms of power: the first form is voice, the second form is exit. You either speak up with your voice, and express your political will to force change. When that doesn't work, you opt for the second vital power that all humans have: exit. Borders have been erected for millenia to prevent exit, to slow down the exit. You can't easily emigrate, opt out, depart, or exit.

What happens when exit is not a physical act, but a virtual act? What happens when people decide to exit from the financial system in a virtual way? VR-exit? Bit-exit?

The insiders can keep the inside of the gilded cage. It is demographically stagnated, over-leveraged, swimming in debt, and out of control. It serves a tiny sliver of the population. They can keep it.

An entire generation of Millennials no longer believe in that fiction of bank security, of deferred earnings, of interest rates and mortgages. They will exit; they are exiting in droves. Not just here, but even more so in the countries where the existing system of insider finance and the system of control are used despotically and oppressively. China is exiting in droves and it has barely started.

Bitcoin has been around for nine years. What does the insider group do? What do the regulators do in response to a system that cannot be regulated? They regulate the bits they can: the exchanges, bank accounts, and national currency side of things. They shut down the on-ramps and off-ramps. They say, "We will not let you take your money with you."

What do Millennials say to that? "Dude… I don't have any money anyway!" "All I have is my creative potential, my spirit, my productivity. I can sell that directly for bitcoin without an exchange, an on-ramp or an off-ramp. When I need to buy something, I will use my digital currency directly without re-entering your system - to which I was never invited. Shut down the on-ramps, shut down the off-ramps. I will stay on board. I will stay digital. I won't touch your gilded cage anymore, because I don't need you. I exit."

Thank you.

Worse Than Useless

The original video presentation of this talk was recorded at the *Baltic Honeybadger Conference* in Riga, Latvia; November 2017. Video Link: https://aantonop.io/WorseThanUseless

First, Do No Harm

The Hippocratic oath, one of the mainstays of medicine, starts with "first, do no harm." It expresses the principle of minimization, the principle of utility. This utilitarian philosophy says that before you try to fix things, make sure you're not making them worse.

Ironically, the father of medicine, Hippocrates, didn't say this. It wasn't part of the Hippocratic oath or Hippocrates' writing. It was added after the introduction of modern science into medicine in the mid 19th century.

"First do no harm." Because some things are not just useless, they're worse than useless. They actually do harm. That is the title of my talk today: "Worse than Useless."

Hippocrates was actually a big proponent of blood-letting, a practice that started in the ancient Mediterranean region. It involved balancing the humours in the body, by bleeding people out slowly. The idea was that the various fluids in the body need to be balanced - like a hydrodynamic system. Before modern science started thinking of our body as more of a machine made of clockwork, which is the 19th and 20th century visualization, the ancients saw it as a matter of essences, of humours. Earth, fire, water, air. The idea of blood-letting was, if these things are out of balance (i.e. you are sick), you need to release some blood to bring things into balance. This practice continued all the way into the 19th century.

One of the most famous victims of blood-letting was a Founding Father of the United States of America: George Washington. Late in his life, George Washington woke up one day with a sore throat. He was a big fan of blood-letting as a medical practice, and invited his doctors / butchers to do a blood-letting. Over the next four days, they bled about seven pints of blood out of him.

The historical record is this: "Despite the treatment, he passed away four days later." Some of us might say, "Because of the treatment, he died four days later."

An Unscientific Method

Why is it important to remember this concept of "do no harm"? If you understand the scientific method, you know that many of the common practices we apply today are based not on science, but on superstition, anecdote, wishful thinking, and righteous morality. One of those practices is financial surveillance, the system of "Know Your Customer" (KYC) and anti-money laundering (AML) rules.

The modern system of banking, brought into being by the Bank Secrecy Act of 1970, is a creation that bears no scrutiny from science. It is based on the righteous moral thinking that bad people should not have access to money, and as long as we trust those in authority to tell us who the bad people are (and assume they themselves are not the bad people), then everything will work out.

If you criticize this idea, you are not presented with facts, data, or science. You are accused of not being morally righteous enough to understand that we must "protect the children." "Won't somebody please think of the children?" Because there are criminals out there. There are "bad people," and if bad people can use money, they might use it to do bad things. It is very difficult to prosecute the bad things, but it is a lot easier to prosecute the money. And so we do it.

Does it work? No.

But if this practice was useless, that would be good. But it is not useless, it is worse than useless. In fact, it does enormous harm. Billions of people around the world have no participation in the world economy and are financially excluded. The practice closes the financial system and authority is given to few to decide who is "good" and who is "evil," who should have access to money and who should not.

A License to Launder

Money laundering happens every day, but there are some who can money launder without consequences. In our modern world, there is such a thing as a license to launder money: it is called a banking license. As long as you have one of these magic licenses, you can launder money all day long. Who is laundering money? Of course, conventional wisdom and common sense will tell you- it is the banks. If you look at the statistics and the data, this fact is proven again and again. Banks have the money; they launder. That is one of their main activities! They launder money for governments, intelligence agencies funding terrorism; they launder money for narco-traffickers.

One of the hilarious examples was a certain big bank that modified their teller windows in one of their branches near the northern border of Mexico precisely so they could fit a Samsonite case (the favourite case of drug money launderers) and conveniently stuff cash through. They wouldn't have to even unpack it. In those days, the big drug cartels were making so much money (and they still are) that they didn't count money. You weigh it, because that is faster. Who has time to count a truck full of money? You can just calculate the net weight.

Money laundering is something that banks do on a routine basis. Every time they're caught, they pay a small fine, no one goes to jail, and profitable banking continues. Signaling that this a fundamental part of their business.

Bankers are rewarded and there are numerous incentives to ensure that so long as they play along with these fake regulations, they can prevent competition in the industry. No one could compete with traditional banking using technology because the regulations ensure competitors will not be given an opportunity. The barriers to entry are too high and you must ask for permission first. The answer is always "no," unless you can afford a banking license, the license to money launder and the fines that come with it as part of doing business. Banks can afford it, because there is one thing banks do well, and that is make a lot of money.

The Real *Dark Net*

The very basis of modern finance is an idea that should be so abhorrent to free people that one would think it would be the topic of every conversation.

We discuss the revelations from Edward Snowden about broad-based surveillance of our societies on the internet. Yet the elephant in the room, the thing we don't discuss, is the most pervasive and intrusive form of surveillance: the international network of totalitarian financial surveillance.

Every time you use a debit card, a credit card, a bank account, the transaction is funneled to intelligence services of governments which surveil these networks.

When people criticize Bitcoin, they often say it will "enable the dark net." What is the dark net? Presumably the "dark net" is invisible to most of us, operates on top of and in parallel with the internet, and massive amounts of illegal activity happen. If that is the case, the dark net's name is ECHELON, PRISM, X-KEYSCORE. Those are the names of the real "dark net." The "dark net" is operated by intelligence agencies because they are, on a daily basis, committing massive crimes against human rights. They orchestrate a totalitarian financial surveillance network that monitors everybody's transactions, location, purchasing preferences, political preferences, and even what kind of porn you watch. All of that is tied to your financial life; everything is tied to your financial life.

This system of totalitarian financial surveillance is the real "dark net." They don't fear the dark net, they just don't want us to have one too.

Privacy vs. Secrecy

Why does Bitcoin matter? Bitcoin enables us to build a system where we can flip the balance between secrecy and privacy.

What is secrecy? What is privacy?

Privacy is what I have, not because someone gives it to me, not because it was granted as a privilege, but because I claim it as my human right. I have had it from birth; I will have it forever. Unfortunately, that is immediately suspicious to some people.

Secrecy is the ability of a government, that is supposed to be subservient to its voters and operating by the consent of the governed, to instead bypass democratic control and accountability. They use it to funnel billions of dollars into highly classified black projects, to fund terrorism and drug lords.

Who funds ISIS? Our tax money does. That is the uncomfortable truth. Not with bitcoin, but with dollars and rubles and yuan. Money laundering is a government-sponsored activity supported by banks. Terrorism financing is a government activity supported by the banks. Yet they have the audacity to claim that people shouldn't be free to transact, participate in a global economy, or exercise their birthright of privacy, because the world will descend into chaos, mayhem, and anarchy.

What happens when people can transact anonymously? Nothing happens. For thousands of years, people were transacting anonymously. The greatest, most established, private and peer-to-peer network of payments is called cash. We've had it for thousands of years. Suddenly, in the 1970s, it became dangerous. We moved to a world of totalitarian financial surveillance. It tries to be all-encompassing, all-powerful, and secret. That is what the word *totalitarian* means. It is fascist.

Somehow, we the people have been persuaded that "for the sake of the children," all of our transactions must be visible, but every one of their transactions is private. I say that is the wrong way around; I say we need to flip that equation and flip it fast.

The reason the world is in chaos is partly because of that system. You want to breed terrorism? Cut people off from the economy, trap them in poverty, and remove justice. What eventually happens is war. Martin Luther King Jr. effectively said, *Peace is not the absence of war, it is the presence of justice.* Justice starts with the assertion of human rights.

Enabling Financial Privacy

Bitcoin is not about playing with money, getting rich, creating a new investment token or the next upper class to lord over everybody else. At least, that is not what I'm interested in. I am interested in creating peace through justice. Justice starts with enabling every human being on this planet to transact freely, with privacy. Anyone, anywhere, anytime. Uncensorable, unstoppable, anonymous.

You think the fight over Bitcoin's block size was bad? You think a few people fighting with trolls and sockpuppets in social media, throwing money around to influence opinion on both sides was bad? There are people who are working on the next upgrades for Bitcoin, including zero-knowledge range proofs, confidential transactions, CoinJoins, and onion routed payment channels which are completely unstoppable.

People ask me, "What do you think is the biggest problem with Bitcoin? Is it scaling? Is it fraud? Is it centralization of mining?"

No, it is that we don't have enough anonymity. We don't have enough privacy. We better fix that before this gets too popular. Adoption of a platform or application with insufficient privacy is extremely dangerous. If you're the only one doing anonymous transactions, you are not anonymous. We need ubiquity of privacy. This should not be an option I enable in my Samourai wallet that says *Use Tor*. It should be default on every wallet, every time. There should be no transaction that isn't confidential.

Here is the interesting thing: if you ask the banks whether they want anonymous transactions, they absolutely do! Some of their "distributed ledger technology" is being built with anonymity, using zero-knowledge proofs, range proofs, mixers, and confidential transactions. They are trying to build confidential and anonymous systems for settlement. Why? Because they can't trust the pompous asshat sitting across the table from them who runs the competitive bank. If they know what happens on the network, they will front-run every transaction, they will pump-and-dump every traded asset. Why? Because that is already what they do every single day. Of course, since they can't trust each other, they understand the need for privacy.

They will build their private blockchains, their clearing and settlement networks. They will make absolutely sure that they have confidentiality, privacy, anonymity, deniability. They will make sure to have all of those things, while still continuing business as usual.

They will achieve their secrecy. The question now is, will we achieve our privacy? Will we assert our human rights? Will we use this technology not to enslave the world through a totalitarian financial system, but to free the world?

Will we do something that, first and foremost, will "do no harm"?

Thank you.

_Publisher's note: At one point in this talk, Martin Luther King Jr. is paraphrased. The quote being referened is: "Peace is not merely the absence of some negative force — war, tension, confusion, but it is the presence of some positive force —justice, goodwill, the power of the kingdom of God." You can find the full sermon, delivered on March 29th 1956, by searching for the *When Peace Becomes Obnoxious* Sermon, and there is an archive of the full text at kinginstitute.stanford.edu

Escaping the Global Banking Cartel

The original video presentation of this talk was recorded as part of Andreas'
The Internet of Money Tour 2018 in Seattle, Washington; November 2018.
Video Link: https://aantonop.io/EscapingCartel

Cartels

What do you call it when a bunch of companies collude to set prices, fix
markets, close off competition, capture regulators, and bribe politicians?
We call it a cartel, right? Like the oil cartel. Have you heard of the term
"cartel"?

Who here has heard of the term *banking cartel*? Oh, we don't hear that term.
We don't talk about the banking cartel. We don't talk about the information
cartel. How many of you here in Seattle work for one of the information
cartel companies? Uh-huh… Big smile on the box?

Cartels are the most insidious when we don't talk about them, when they
hide in the shadows but in plain view. The banking system, payments,
finance are the biggest cartels in the world. Nobody calls them a cartel
because they're the biggest cartel in the world. They own all of the media
channels, politicians and laws; that makes it easy for them to get away with
crimes. In fact, mega-crimes.

Robo-Signing

Just after the crisis in 2008, instead of some bankers going to jail, they set
up an additional layer of crime: a series of fraudulent foreclosures called
robo-signing. Maybe you remember that crisis. One of the lead companies
in that space, the biggest robo-signer of all, was run by a guy called Steven
Mnuchin. Does anybody know what that guy does today? He is the Treasury
Secretary of the United States. Apparently he can do that job without
running it from a jail cell. He got a sweet deal, he didn't have to accept any
wrong-doing, and then quickly got a cozy job. Now he has the ultimate level
of protection, which is qualified immunity. That is how cartels work.

First they capture the market. Then they capture the regulators, who claim
to care deeply about consumer protection. The regulator is there to protect
against evil things happening. For example, money laundering. If you don't

have a banking license, no money laundering for you! But if you do have a banking license… Well, I mean we must protect "the system." There will be a fine. Usually the fine will be less than what you made actually laundering money. You will get away with it, right? Of course, we don't want to see any financing of terrorists… except for the ones we do through the State Department, the CIA, or the banks — in which case, those are good people. They are captured.

Crony Capitalism

That kind of situation encourages behaviours that are fundamentally parasitic. When capitalism fails in this particular mode, when you end up with full-blown crony capitalism, it is also known as kleptocracy. Kleptocracy is from the Greek word *klepto,* which means thief, and *krátos* which means power. The thieves are in power, literally. That is kleptocracy, when the most parasitic behaviours get rewarded. When you run a business at that scale, it is not actually about competing. It is about finding the biggest pipe, the biggest flow of money in the economy, straddling that pipe, sticking a straw in it, and sucking as much of that money out as you can.

When you are a large player in the banking cartel, you can establish yourself as a parasitic leech on a flow of money. The idea is, you find a job that requires an intermediary; of course, it requires an intermediary because you made sure to buy some lawyers to write a law and some lobbyists to persuade Congress to adopt that law. You made sure that the law requires an intermediary (specifically, you). Then you stick a straw into that flow of money and start extracting rents. It's called rent-seeking behavior. You take half a percentage point here, half a percentage point there. You provide little to no value to those paying the rent.

We have this wonderful thing called fractional reserve banking. If you're unfamiliar with fractional reserve banking, the gist of it is that commercial banks take one dollar and create another nine dollars out of thin air. If you explained that to a five-year-old, they would probably turn around and say, "That sounds like fraud!" They would be right. Of course, there is a big difference between something that sounds like fraud and something that is legal. The big difference is too often the size of the check.

We have these parasitic companies, sitting on top of these flows of money, extracting rent. They created this rent-seeking behavior and in doing so, they disrupt competition by buying and suing competitors, or even better — making sure that competitors can't keep up with regulation. They capture regulators to keep the competition at bay. In doing that, they have built a cartel.

Then they make sure nobody calls it a cartel. Instead, we call it "the shining example of American capitalism." The end result of this is appalling. Obviously, it's not a good model for an economy and it's certainly not a free market.

When Money Stops Working

But who does it really hurt? Does it matter if a bunch of people get obscenely rich without having to compete? Does it really matter?

Well, to most people in a semi-functioning thriving economy, it doesn't matter. That is the magic. Until money breaks, part of the benefit of freedom, the premium of liberty, is the ability to not give a shit about how any of it works. You don't need to worry about these details; you live in a free country. You're free to instead pay attention to Sunday football, enjoy your life, and have another hot dog.

But when money stops working, suddenly all of it comes crashing back. You have to start learning some new vocabulary. At the end of 2008, we all had to start learning.

"Grandma, what is a credit default swap?" "I don't know. Let's ask Uncle John. He has a degree in finance." "He doesn't know either."

Half of the people in finance didn't know what a credit default swap was, how it worked, or what was hiding behind it. Suddenly, everyone needed to know what a credit default swap was, because apparently it chewed a giant hole right in the middle of the economy. When money stops working, everything stops working. Then you're on a crash course to learn whose fault it was.

Re-writing History

There are two alternative histories. In one of these histories, there were some oopsies. Some things happened. People made some bad mistakes. But, you know… they are just people trying to do their job. In the end, it was mostly the fault of greedy homeowners who didn't read the fine print carefully enough, to realize they were buying a ballooning interest rate. They had the audacity to want to own a home. Because of these greedy people, the real-estate market had an oopsie.

But don't worry! The irresponsible people had their homes taken away from them. The banks got some cash infusions, which we don't want to talk about too much… Everything was fixed, we passed some laws, and it will not happen again. Really, it was just a blip. In the next ten years, we will just rebuild everything. Everybody is happy. Now we have a roaring economy that is working great! That is the first story.

The second story may be familiar to more of you, who are probably in the middle class. They robbed us blind, strip-mined the economy, had an orgy of fraud, and knew exactly what they were doing. There are mountains and mountains of evidence that the least competent RICO lawyer could use to unravel the entire thing and send five hundred people to jail for twenty-five years. That was ignored because we must save the system. Otherwise, the system would crush us all.

We dumped more than $10 trillion in a binge of quantitative easing into the banks, which they did not use to stimulate any part of the economy, but instead to blow another giant bubble into real-estate, into the stock market, into bonds, into student loans, into subprime auto loans, into every part of the economy.

Meanwhile, they made sure those cops beat the shit out of those who had the audacity to protest as part of Occupy Wall Street. That didn't work. They turned protest into a crime. They didn't just damage the economy, they raped the rule of law in this country and manipulated the justice system so they could get away with it.

Destroying the Rule of Law

We have come full circle today. Ten years later, where are we? Ten trillion dollars in debt, ten more giant bubbles. It will happen again, because a system like that is fragile and corrupt; it is architected in such a way as to reward and encourage that kind of behavior. In a system of incentives where the penalty is less than the profits you made by committing the crime, that is legal immunity. That is a very loud signal, in a system of crony capitalism, that says, "Do it again. Only this time, leverage more! We could probably squeeze out another ten years."

When the result of saving the system is the destruction of people's livelihoods, they rage. Usually, that rage gets misdirected. There is an old adage of the rich guy who has ninety-nine cookies, the middle-class having one cookie, and the rich guy saying to them, "Watch it! That peasant will take your cookie." That is the oldest trick in the game.

One of the houses stolen by Steven Mnuchin's robo-signing firm belonged to the guy — I won't name him because he doesn't deserve to be named — who sent mail bombs to critics of Trump and government offices in the USA just a couple of weeks ago. That guy was robo-closed by Steven Mnuchin and turned his rage against immigrants, gays, and Democrats. Why? I don't know. The point is, when you have financial and wealth destruction in a society, when you destroy the rule of law and create rage among people, they don't know where to turn. What you get is violence, extremism, bigotry, hatred and a desperate desire to find someone to blame.

Of course, you can't really hold Mnuchin and others like him accountable. They are behind very tall walls with very good security. The guillotines are out of fashion. They tried that in France, but we can't do it again because we are now a civilized country.

So what do you do? Protest? That ends in a spree of violence by militarised police, exactly what police have always done. You can't do that. Occupy? That was tried. Again, a spree of violence. A lot of young voters tried apathy. "I don't give a shit. These old people fucked it up. I will just go and play my game and ignore all of this." That doesn't work out very well. Trying to become part of the parasitic class by clawing your way to just escape from the middle class? Well, there is a tide of shit right behind you and it is moving faster than you are. The middle class is sliding backwards so fast that, while you try to scramble out of it, you are still backsliding, so that doesn't work.

Change the Architecture

How do we fix this problem? The first thing we need to do is identify why this keeps happening. In my opinion, looking at this from a technology perspective, architecture is at the core of the problem. An architecture of hierarchy and centralization is responsible for this. Parasitic behavior gets rewarded because there are centralized flows of money that someone can tap into. We have taken the traditional model of commerce — where you visit, interact, and trade with other people around you in your community, a system of peer-to-peer commerce — and we have converted it into a system that I call a peer-to-corporation- to-corporation-to-peer system. When I pay my butcher, Visa, Chase, and three other banks get involved. They all stick a little straw in that flow. By the time the money reaches my butcher, it is a lot less.

How can you make a system like that work? It is absurd. You would need to create a sense of apathy, combined with the convenience of waving a piece of plastic. You would need to create a dark cloud over cash ("terrorists!") and pretend it is something we should get rid of, because people might use it to evade taxes. Of course, the people who evade taxes use corporations, very expensive lawyers, and actually get away with it. But the butcher might evade some taxes if we use cash, so we'll eradicate cash?

That hierarchy is not just poisonous for the system of commerce that we have. It is not just our banking system. It becomes a haven for parasites because the very architecture itself concentrates power, creates a reward system for parasitic behavior.

This is now happening with information cartels.

"Let's take everyone's identity, put it in a big pot, place Mark Zuckerberg on top of the pot, and- Oops, we fucked up our electoral system." *"But we have cat videos!"* "Hey, democracy is dying-" *"But we have cat videos!"*

That is okay, is it?

The Hidden Costs of Convenience

The information cartels, the payment cartels, and the electoral system are so centralized, that the Secretary of State in Georgia can run for governor and be in charge of elections and voter registration at the same time. We have electronic voting machines making it so quick that you can count the votes incorrectly in an hour, instead of counting them correctly over three days. We have convenience. You can tap on the screen to vote, but the system changes your vote to something else, and it is still counted, instantly! Convenience! And democracy dies a little.

We have the liberty to ignore most of these remote negative side-effects that arise out of centralization. In this country we have an incredible amount of economic momentum and a dirty deal with the Saudis to sell oil only for U.S. dollars. That ensures we will continue to have low interest rates and the rest of the world will buy treasury bonds. We can maintain a lifestyle of convenience. The illusion that this will continue to work, allows us to accept this behaviour, and not try too hard to change it. We're not in a panic. It's not an emergency. It was in 2008, but that was "fixed." "Don't worry. It will not happen again," they say. But we didn't actually fix anything, so next time it will be even bigger. The same symptoms still exist, but don't worry, they say.

While you're not worrying, someone in Argentina is worrying because their currency just crashed 45%. They are experiencing that this year in an accelerated fashion, in an environment where they can't simply outsource their debt to the rest of the world in exchange for oil and war. They suffer the consequence immediately. It is happening in Venezuela, and in Brazil again. It is happening in Turkey, in Ukraine, and in dozens of other countries.

Until now, in all of these countries, when your esteemed leader said your currency was crashing and your economy was dying, they tried to claim that it was not because of systemic corruption throughout the entire system, or the parasitic behaviour of hierarchies sucking off the middle class, feasting on the carcass of the economy. They claimed it was sabotage by the foreigners next door, or some other external threat. And not only is it your patriotic duty to use the currency, but it is also your patriotic duty to not leave the country. Of course, refugees do all the time, so apparently they are not patriotic.

An Exit Door

Until 2008, there wasn't really an alternative, there was no exit.

Holding U.S. dollars as a foreign currency, hoarding gold, or putting it under your mattress, that is easy for a government to stop, to break down and censor. They can confiscate your gold and raid your house. If you are seen exchanging hard(er) currency, like foreign currency, with others, you could get shot. You won't just have a misdemeanor fine. Countries take entire populations hostage in these hyperinflation spirals.

Then something happened in 2008: Bitcoin. For the first time in modern history, there was another option. That option isn't just a separate currency. It is a currency that can't be easily confiscated, that can easily be transmitted across borders, that can be used as a lifeboat by people who can't physically exit the country. They can exit the economy virtually, trading in another currency right where they are, creating a parallel micro-economy in their community which becomes connected to other little lifeboats. Life can continue past the crisis. They don't have to go down with the sinking boat of state to be patriotic.

That is happening today in Venezuela, in Argentina and in Turkey. Before that, in Cyprus and other places. It is happening again and again, as people discover they have some other options. Today, too few people can effectively exit. It requires a level of literacy, numeracy, and technological confidence that is not yet present in the masses. But think about what happens in twenty years when some dictator decides to take an entire economy hostage, and 25% of the population says, "Bye! I'm taking my money out now."

Taking their money out isn't the act of investment like we see here in the United States. People say, "Let's invest in bitcoin," as if it is some kind of stock. "Let's buy low, sell high. Let's make lots of money, get rich quick!"

Instead, the act of exit is to say, "I will take my productive capital, my labor, my services, my products, and I will make them available for this currency. I am simultaneously entering a new economy, trading with other people who are with me, and I have exited. I have withdrawn my participation, my collaboration, from a system that is broken." On that basis alone, this is a technology that will change the world. But that's not what it's all about.

Decentralization

You've probably heard the term decentralization. Especially when you talk with others about cryptocurrencies or open blockchains. To most people, decentralization doesn't really mean anything. It is a vague word that doesn't have any impact in their lives.

Let's decipher what decentralization means.

Decentralization in its purest form means peer-to-peer, edge-to-edge, end-to-end, and removing intermediaries. It means reconnecting with each other so that we can have transactions, interactions. Not just with money, but also with trust, corporate governance, and other things that could be enabled through smart contracts. We can now do these things without intermediaries.

What role do intermediaries serve? In most cases and markets, the fundamental purpose of an intermediary is two-fold: To provide a way for two parties (such as a buyer and a seller) to engage in any kind of trusted transaction to find each other. Intermediaries create conditions where people can find each other. That is what Uber does. The drivers are out there; you're out there. What is it Uber is doing? They are helping you find each other. That is a good function, but we could also do that with just software.

Why exactly, in this day and age, do we need to create these double-ended markets where people need to find each other? Trust. I can't trust the driver unless there is some way of validating their reliability, through some kind of review or previous experience. The driver can't trust that I will actually pay them. Trust, until 2009, was a function that could only be done by intermediaries acting in a hierarchy of oversight. "I trust this intermediary because it is overseen by another intermediary, who is overseen by another..." The theory goes, eventually overseen by someone who is a representative, in some elected body, where I have some influence within the consent of the governed. The intermediary works for me, through my representatives, and are trusted because they have oversight. Or at least I will have some recourse if my trust was misplaced.

In practice, that is not what happens. In practice, the intermediary gets powerful enough to start buying the intermediaries around and above them. They become bigger and bigger, start sucking and extracting more rent out of the system, until eventually they buy the people doing the oversight. Now the Congressperson works for them, and I am not a part of the system anymore. It is no longer peer-to-peer. It is peer- to-corporation-to-corporation-to-peer. We're out.

Disintermediation

Recently someone asked, "If a homeless person on the street asks you for a donation, how do you pay with bitcoin? You can't pay them with bitcoin!" Actually, I can and I have. I takes fifteen minutes. I must teach them how to install a wallet, where to spend it, and how to find other people. It becomes an exercise of slightly patronizing education, of course, but sometimes it is worth it. I will also give them some cash because I'm not a monster. Deciding to tip at restaurants or give money to homeless people only in bitcoin is heartless. But as far as giving them bitcoin, it's really quite simple.

My question back to this person was, "Tell me, how do you pay the homeless person with a credit card? How many of you are carrying that much cash, that you use for any purpose other than tipping? We don't. We have outsourced our commerce through these intermediaries. I have a simple question for you.

In this room tonight, how many of you have a point-of-sale merchant system that can accept a credit card? I do. I count two, three, four, five, six, seven, eight, nine out of 380 people. Almost none of you can accept my credit card for payment. None of us can take a payment directly using credit cards. We must use intermediaries. Not just one. They're stacked together to make a little pyramid of intermediaries. You might be able to pay me, using your credit card, with PayPal. In that case, PayPal, Visa, and Chase bank (for example) could all be involved. But did you notice they didn't actually *do* anything. What did they do? They moved some bits on the internet! We have been moving bits on the internet for twenty-five years, practically for free! How did they figure out that this costs 2% of my transaction?

Perhaps the greatest thing the internet has done for us can be summarized in one word: disintermediation.

Do I need to put a classified ad in a newspaper to sell my furniture to my neighbor? Oh no, I don't. Bye-bye, newspapers. Oops, they're gone! An industry that existed for hundreds of years, now a hollow shell that does info-tainment. Several other industries have gradually fallen to this powerful effect of disintermediation.

Disintermediation is important because it allows you to do two things: shorten the distance between buyers and sellers, and remove points of friction or control. It means lower costs, faster service, a more direct interaction between the service provider and the person consuming it. We can start behaving like human beings that interact with each other. If I buy from someone directly, I know who they are. We don't need three intermediaries of trust between us. Disintermediation removes them.

Breaking the System-of-Control

The other insidious problem of intermediaries is control. They not only take a cut of everything they are involved with, but they also start telling you what you can and cannot sell, to whom you can and cannot sell, in which country you can and cannot send money. That might be okay if they shared my moral principles and decided, *No, we shouldn't be sending 40% of our budget to Lockheed Martin and General fucking Dynamics to bomb people around the world. Maybe we should do something else.* But no, they don't have my moral principles, or probably your moral principles either.

They think it's very wrong to send money to WikiLeaks, which hasn't been convicted of doing anything wrong - ever! But it's perfectly all right to send a contribution to the Alabama chapter of the Ku Klux Klan (KKK).

A fundamental problem of our platforms today is that these intermediaries are gatekeepers. The side effect is not just the 2% cost of every transaction; it is the erosion of democracy. It is the destruction of all other institutions we used to have control over. We no longer have a choice, we no longer have a voice. What is left when you have no choice, no voice?

Exit.

We can exit the hard way, try to get fifty people into a tiny boat and across the Mediterranean, a man-made crisis. But exit the slightly less hard way, is saying "I'm opting out. I am leaving your centralized, parasitical system. I am choosing to use decentralized platforms for my money, my payments. Perhaps, in the future, also for my speech, my publishing, my corporate organization, and other trusted interactions." Trust used to be a function of hierarchy. It no longer is. Trust is now a protocol.

When we have the technological tools to convert trusted institutions into a peer-to-peer protocol, we take back that control. We remove the intermediaries. We cut off the flows. If you want to stop a parasite, you must stop feeding it first. That is what this is about. That is why decentralization matters.

When I talk to audiences in Argentina, Greece, Cyprus, and other places around the world where they are not part of the 5% population that has our advantages, they understand. They have already seen the consequences, two or three times in one generation. They have seen what happens when money fails, when institutions get corrupted, eroded, and finally destroyed, by these parasitic organisations. These parasitic organizations keep arising because nothing has changed in the fundamental architecture. If the architecture is a pyramid, someone will climb to the top. Changing people at the top doesn't change the architecture. Corruption will flow upwards.

The Weakness of "Don't Be Evil"

Corporations are not immoral, they are amoral. They are machines that only move in one direction, without guidance for morality, because they don't have morals. The people at the top see a big pipe of money, ready to throw millions or billions of dollars into something, anything really, and they want a piece. They stick a straw in it.

"How do we increase our profit margin this week?" "Well, we could sell facial recognition technology to law enforcement. After all what are they going to do with it?" "Hey, didn't Oakland PD murder a whole bunch of their own fucking citizens, even though they were unarmed?" "Yes, but if they violate the Constitution, they will probably be in violation of our Terms of Service. So we can shut them down."

Who the hell do you think you're kidding? Really?

You cannot stop these things by saying, "Be better, Amazon! Be better people. Don't be evil!" What a great slogan. But you can't fix it that way. We need to stop feeding the parasite. We have to change the fundamental architecture. The reason these crimes can be done by large corporations is because of centralization. They have taken the convenience of the one-click buy, the profile share, and all the micro-violations of privacy. They have built a massive information cartel that delivers billions of dollars, that allows them to centralize and become parasites. They are actually quite benevolent right now. But we know where this is going. It will not get better. It will not magically resolve itself until we change the fundamental architecture.

Peer-to-Peer Architecture

The reason Bitcoin is so strongly resisted by those who run the current architecture is because it says, "We don't need your permission. Your regulation isn't working. You can't scale to solve the problems of this planet. At a very fundamental level, your architecture is wrong."

The architecture we want is peer-to-peer, flat, decentralized, and end-to-end. Innovations are at the edges, without permission, and are part of everyone's experience. Peer-to-peer architecture matters — in money, corporate governance, law, and voting.

But first and most importantly, we have to starve the parasites. The first thing we need to break is the cartel of money. We do that by exiting, by using peer-to-peer money.

Thank you.

Bitcoin: A Swiss Bank in Everyone's Pocket

The original video presentation of this talk was recorded at Andreas' *The Internet of Money Tour 2019*. This event was hosted by the Swiss Bitcoin Association in Zurich, Switzerland; June 2019. Video Link: https://aantonop.io/SwissBank

Community Builders

Hello everyone, it's lovely to see all of you! It is so much fun to be in Zurich again. The last time I was in Zurich, I did a talk for a Swiss bankers association. There were a lot more suits in that room. When I see too many suits in a room, I feel really uncomfortable. 'Are they trying to sell me something? Is this a funeral? What just happened?' I am very happy that today we have a lot of people from the community. It looks like the entire community turned up. Thank you so much for coming tonight. I heard that this is now the largest meetup event that has happened in Europe on the topic of open blockchains. Thanks so much for giving me trust and coming out for this event.

Today's event is supported by my patrons. This is part of a seven-city tour; the last five cities in this tour are all community events that are free to attend. The only reason I can do that is because my work is funded by the community directly, through donations. We will be releasing this video first on Patreon, then to everyone else on YouTube. I'll be doing a Question and Answer session tonight after my talk, but I also do a monthly Q&A session for community builders on Patreon, in case you can't get your question answered tonight.

Forget About Libra

The title of my talk is a complete diversion. I am not really going to talk about 'Thoughts on the Future of Programmable Money.' If you have seen a few of my presentations, you already know this trick. Every time I deliver a talk, it is improvisation. I talk about a topic that I decide on the same day. The problem is, months before the event, the organizers are asking me, "What are you going to talk about." I say, "I don't know." "But we need a title!" So I thought, 'What is the most generic title possible that allows me to talk about absolutely anything?' Thoughts on the Future of Programmable Money.

That is not what I'm going to talk about tonight. I am also not going to talk about Libra. Because guess what? Even with a topic as broad as 'Thoughts on the Future of Programmable Money,' Libra doesn't really fit. It is not money or really programmable. I don't know if it has a future. I do have some thoughts. We recorded a couple of 'Let's Talk Bitcoin' shows on the topic of Libra. I also did a talk in Edinburgh, which we will release soon. If you want to hear my thoughts on that, it will come up. I'm sure the very first question in our Q&A is going to be about that. We will discuss it then, but I don't want to talk about it tonight. Tonight, there's something else.

The Encryption Debate

Let's talk about "good" and "bad" technology.

In 2016, President Barack Obama said something amazing at the South by Southwest festival. He was talking about 'unbreakable encryption,' but the quote applies here. He said that using encryption would be as if "everybody is walking around with a Swiss Bank account in their pocket." Yeah? Little did he know, that is a fantastic advertisement for cryptocurrency. Exactly. It would be as if everybody had a Swiss bank account in their pocket.

Of course, he didn't mean it as something positive, as something that we should all be excited about. He was fear-mongering. "Uh! Imagine if everybody could have a Swiss bank account in their pocket." Not just his friends, or all of the other people in Congress. Not just the lobbyists and executives who pay for his campaigns. Not just all of the weapons manufacturers and all of the other people he talks to, but everyone! 'Ugh! Those people.'

Of course, Barack Obama was wrong. Crypto is not like having a Swiss bank account in your pocket. Crypto is like having a Swiss bank in your pocket, and you are the CEO. On your wallet, you can create a million addresses, like accounts, on your little phone. You can authorize the equivalent of international wire transfers. You can KYC yourself. "Know Your Customer? A pretty handsome guy, I see him in the mirror every morning… I know him. Who is he sending to? My best friend. I know him too. KYC done!"

You can have a bank account in your pocket. With it, you can engage in some of the activities that banks do. For example, money laundering. Three years ago, I put a pair of my favourite jeans in the washing machine. I kid you not, I had my hardware wallet in the front pocket. This was a very well-designed piece of hardware, because it went through a whole wash cycle, a spin cycle, and even went in the dryer. I pulled it out and thought, 'There is no way that this will still work.' But it did work. So, money laundering? Done! I have achieved something in my life that most people can only do by being a banker, or knowing a banker.

The Politics of Fear

What Barack Obama said came from the politics of fear. Of course, he is not the only one, right? Every single politician is singing the same tune. The idea is, privacy in the hands of the people is dangerous. Because privacy has become a commodified right. Some people can afford it; for the rest, the price of privacy has risen outside of affordability. Politicians and their friends have privacy because they can afford it.

Look at what happens when someone blows the whistle, tells their secrets. Look at how the politicians react. Look at what is happening to Julian Assange right now. To Chelsea Manning. To Thomas Drake. To John Kiriakou. If you don't know those names, look them up.

When our government commits war crimes, the only person going to jail is the one who told the journalist that the government is committing war crimes. Yours too, right? When there is a scandal in the government, the person most likely to go to jail is the person who published something about it. "But they are not a journalist," they say. "They are not a journalist"? Guess what. Journalism is not a thing you are licensed for. It is not just a job description. As the saying goes, "A journalist is one who commits acts of journalism." That is who a journalist is. Anyone who commits acts of journalism is a journalist. Julian Assange is a journalist who is being persecuted for breaking the secrecy of very powerful people.

Do you have privacy? Hell, no. Because you would be "criminals." I mean, you do look like criminals to me, especially that guy right there. *Audience laughs.*

We are constantly being pushed by politicians to fear privacy. To fear what happens when we democratize privacy. That is what we are talking about here. The democratization of finance is also about the democratization of privacy, financial privacy. Financial privacy underpins all of our other human rights: freedom of expression, assembly, and association. Political participation. Travel. Due-process. Just ask the people in Hong Kong who are buying train tickets with cash, because they know that the last time they went to a protest, half of them were rounded up by the government because they used their smartcards. Not so smart anymore, right? Give me good old paper and cash.

Privacy is a fundamental human right. Financial privacy and power are things that we, through our participation in events like this tonight, are seizing back. That right is not given to us; we have always had it. We have the right to exercise our financial privacy. We are simply taking it back. In many cases, it wasn't even taken from us. Some of our neighbors and relatives, in fear, gave it away to the government. They conceded this right.

The idea that, if people have financial privacy, the world will descend into chaos, is nonsense. For thousands of years, we have had peer-to-peer anonymous transactions. Cash or barter transactions weren't tracked. The world did not descend into chaos. In fact, many of the greatest achievements in civilization happened before the era of financial surveillance. Yet now we must be fearful?

The Asymmetry of Good and Evil

Underlying the politics of fear is a refusal to recognize the asymmetry of good and evil. The fact is, in human society, the number of people who do evil is tiny. To equivocate about the number of people who do good is to ignore human nature. When we engage in the politics of fear in order to punish the few people doing evil, we punish everybody. We remove the capability for financial independence and sovereignty from everyone. Worse, we give those capabilities and the power of surveillance to a government. What kind of people does that very powerful government attract? The very evil people we're talking about.

There are more people trying to do good with their financial independence and empowerment than there are trying to do evil. That asymmetry is at the core of classical liberalism. The more free people are, the more good outcomes you will have in society. You should trust people to pursue their own self-interest. The pursuit of happiness, as we used to call it in America. If you allow people to do that, they will seek a better life for themselves, for their children, and for their neighbors. That is human nature.

We are walking away from that and creating a world where we are trying to control everyone. In doing so, we are damaging the possibility for a better future.

The Remedy for Bad Speech

In 1927, Supreme Court Justice Louis Brandeis said that the remedy for bad speech is more speech. I am paraphrasing, but that was the essence of what he said. If you have bad speech, you should allow others to correct the misinformation and fallacies. Allow the truth to come forth. Remedy bad speech with more good speech.

The remedy for evil things that can be done with technology is not less technology; it is more good technology. For every bad thing that you can do with these technologies, you can do more things that are good. You can even counteract some of the bad things by helping more people do good things.

When our governments, regulators, and institutions — which are barely democratic to begin with anymore — try to control the use of technology, they are reducing the number of people who can use it to do good and counteract the evil of the few. Guess what? The people who are doing bad things with this technology will not stop because you passed a law.

If you make it illegal to trade in cryptocurrencies, only criminals will. Probably the very same government ministers who signed the law will be the first criminals to trade in cryptocurrency. They will probably take bribes in cryptocurrency too. They like the idea of having a Swiss bank account in their pocket.

Imagine a world in which everyone could have a Swiss bank account in their pocket. The bad guys already do. They have banking privacy because they can afford it. If it is not in Switzerland, it is in Panama. If it is not in Panama, then it is Malta. If it is not in Malta, then it is Hong Kong. It will be somewhere else next. The bad guys already have these tools. They are breaking the law because they can afford to. What is one more law to them? Nothing.

The solution to dictators evading sanctions with cryptocurrency, is citizens evading dictators with cryptocurrency. There are a hell of a lot more citizens who need to evade dictators than there are dictators evading sanctions. We should be airdropping the technology to use cryptocurrencies. We should be flying B-52s that empty their cargo bays full of hardware wallets, satellite dishes, and Raspberry Pis over North Korea and Venezuela. Because Kim Jong-un already has a bank account down the street. So why don't we give every one of the citizens a Swiss bank in their pocket?

Beyond Cynicism

Governments fear that people will use cryptocurrency to evade taxes. The corporations and politicians already evade taxes. They're concerned about us lowly citizens not paying taxes, because there won't be enough money to provide citizens with services. But there are other ways to fund services. We can come together with our neighbors and raise money for the products, companies, facilities, and services that we want.

In any case, the idea of the majority of citizenry not paying taxes is a really cynical view. The countries with the least amount of bureaucracy involved in paying taxes, and where governments actually deliver services, have the highest levels of tax collection. It is not because you are afraid to go to jail that you pay taxes here in Switzerland, it is because you actually get something in return. What do I get in return for my taxes in the United States? It sure as hell isn't healthcare.

Or roads. The classic question: who will build the roads if we stop paying taxes? All I have to say is, visit Michigan in the winter and tell me about the roads. I don't think the Romans had much trouble building roads when money was anonymous gold transacted hand-to-hand. They kind of invented the idea.

The Remedy for Bad Technology

Bad technology is only countered with greater use of good technology. But for every problem we have in cryptocurrency, regulators are eager to try to solve it. Want consumer protection? Along comes a regulator who says,

"Let's create a committee that builds a regulatory framework for oversight-" Shut up!

Instead we'll do smart contracts with escrow for consumer protection. How about we don't try to solve problems in 21st century technology with an organization from the 18th century that is full of corruption and regulatory capture?

Are you worried about people stealing crypto? Regulators answer, "Great! Let's create a system where we can reverse all of the transactions on the blockchain-" Shut up! No!

We'll use multi-signature, multi-factor, timelocks, vaulting, and convenance. We can fix the problems that are created by the introduction of any new technology, with new technology. We didn't arrive at this modern world we live in by saying, "You know what? Cars are great, but they would be even better if we used horses to pull them. There would be less pollution." If you think that is funny, it was actually suggested at the time. You can see photos of it.

For every problem, we have a solution that requires faith in human nature, and an understanding that most people will use that technology to do good at an asymmetric scale. There are more people in the world who want to do good.

Not All Governments...

You might think, 'But I'm in Switzerland. What are you talking about? I don't have a corrupt government that is stealing from me. I have access to banking, and pretty nice banking too. I don't need to hide my money from the government. I am not ruled by a dictator. We have a great system of not just representative but direct democracy, with propositions and a federal election system.' That's great, fantastic even. If only everybody had a system like that. If only everybody had the level of financial access that you have in Switzerland. But everybody doesn't.

The question then is, why do you need crypto? This is a question that comes up a lot. In Venezuela, Argentina, North Korea, half of sub-saharan Africa, Southeast Asia, and certainly in China, people need crypto. It is a matter of life and death. It is matter of freedom from slavery. It is about a future for their children or nothing. They need crypto, you don't.

You've Got The Power

So why would you use it? Let me tell you why. Every time you use crypto, you are exercising sovereign power that is diverting money from a corrupt and broken system of central banks, investment banks, and governments, into a system that is giving people hope. Every time you use crypto, you are helping to fund the projects that make wallets and decentralized exchanges better; you are helping to fund new innovation and research. How many people here are developers who work in Bitcoin and other open blockchains? The rest of you are paying these people to do better work. Every time you use crypto, you are exercising power.

The greatest lie this generation has been taught to believe, is the idea that we don't have power, or that our power is meaningless. That the enormous problems which exist in the world cannot be solved because we are too small. Our power is too limited. We have all been persuaded that we can only exercise our power once every four years, maybe every two years, even if you are in Switzerland. We all do the little civic dance and go to the polls, which the U.S. does not schedule on a holiday — because who wants people to actually vote? This is a democracy, people. We cast our ballot for one of the two possible candidates. You know, blue Goldman Sachs or red Goldman Sachs. Then we get a little sticker that says, "I voted!" Yet we go home and feel that none of it made any difference. Because on every important issue of the day, the political parties have very comfortably made sure that no one will challenge the status-quo. So none of it matters.

You can sit back and say, "I have no power." You can try to exercise power once every two years, once every four years. Or you could realize that we have all of the power. We could exercise it not once every four years, but 1,200 times every four years by choosing to use and fund open financial products. By sharing with the world education about open financial products, to build a new economy, while simultaneously withdrawing our labor, creativity, and passion from the broken shitty economy we're stuck in. Pour all of that creativity into the open financial future we're building. Exercise that power once per day.

If all of us in this room do it, we change Switzerland. If all of us in the world do it, we change the world. We have enormous power. So what if you don't need it? You have the immense privilege of already possessing these financial products, which are life and death for so many others. Take that privilege and use it to exercise enormous power, to create an open financial future for the entire world, today.

Thank you!

Unstoppable Code: The Difference Between Can't and Won't

The original video presentation of this talk was recorded at the *ETH Denver Event* in Denver, Colorado; February 2019. Video Link: https://aantonop.io/UnstoppableCode

Thank You!

Tonight I won't be talking about *Mastering Ethereum*, except for one thing. I'd like to say 'Thank You' to the dozen or so people in this room who contributed to that book. I don't know if you know the story, but if you don't, I worked hard to make the technical books that I publish through O'Reilly open-source, which is something they don't do with all of their books. Not just open-source eventually, but from the beginning. You can download my O'Reilly books from GitHub, and read them for free. Of course, you can also buy them.

Most importantly, I had the freedom and privilege to write my book as a collaborative project in the true spirit of open-source. I am a big believer in the Creative Commons. That is one of the things we have which none of the competition has. By "we," I mean the entire open-source community around cryptocurrencies. We don't suffer from the tragedy of the commons with closed, proprietary systems. We celebrate a festival of the commons through our collaboration and creativity. When I do my work, I know that I am standing on the shoulders of thousands of other people who have put their passion and creativity into building what I had the privilege of trying to explain in my books. That is a collaborative process.

Mastering Ethereum had 180 contributors, who pushed more than eight thousand commits, submitting more than one thousand pull requests and issues as well. More than a dozen of those people are in this room today. Thanks so much to all of you. You know who you are. Thank you!

Cryptography as a Defensive Technology

The topic we're going to talk about is a bit touchy, it's the topic of unstoppable code. I bring a certain perspective because I started with

Bitcoin, and have been fascinated by the cypherpunk ethos since the early 1990s. Yeah, I am that old.

Part of that ethos is about using cryptography as a defense mechanism in order to claim, assert, and enforce our human rights. It is about using the magic of numbers, not offensively but purely defensively. To an individual, it brings an awesome power that rivals even the state or the most fearsome conglomerates. The totalitarian governments in the world can kiss my 256-bit key, but they won't be able to brute-force it. It doesn't matter how annoyed, angry, or violent they are with what I said, signed, or paid for. Cryptography gives individuals this ability to assert power and sovereignty to create the conditions that allow them to express and enforce human rights.

I strongly believe in these things. I believe in freedom of expression and speech. I believe in creating diverse environments where we all have powers that can't be taken away from us.

The Tension between Governance and Unstoppable Code

What fascinated me about Ethereum from the very beginning was this idea of unstoppable code. You may have heard the slogan, "unstoppable code"; they were the first two words on the website during launch. I think it reflects a lot on the people who were involved in this project early on, the same idea that also makes me interested in Bitcoin and got me started on this journey. The idea of uncensorable speech, not because you asked nicely or anyone likes what you said, but because they simply can't stop you from saying it. That is a very powerful thing, more necessary than ever in today's world. We are gradually sliding into crisis after crisis. We are seeing a rise of totalitarianism. It has never been more important to give people all over the world the tools to express themselves, assert their rights, and to be sovereign.

Right now, most of the Ethereum space is this beautiful wellspring of creativity, passion, and joy. I love it. Unicorns, bufficorns, puppies and rainbows; the sense of limitless possibilities. Unfortunately, it will not last. What we are doing here is important. It seizes power on behalf of individuals from the dominant forms of power: governments, corporations, state associations, cultures, and religions. It seizes power from these big entities and gives it to little people. But sooner or later, the people who are losing their undeserved, abusively applied power in this equation will start fighting back. At that point, we will find out how unstoppable the code is.

What kind of code needs to be unstoppable? What code do we need to build that is unstoppable? Just like with free speech, the only speech that needs protecting is that which deeply offends. Innocuous speech does not require protection. In some cases, it doesn't even deserve it. "Journalism is about publishing what people don't want you to publish; everything else is public relations." Have you heard that quote? The only speech worth protecting is the speech people don't want to hear, and the only code that needs to be unstoppable is the code that someone is trying to stop. That is worthwhile. That is exciting.

Governance is a killer app for Ethereum. Unstoppable code is also a killer app, but between them there is a subtle tension. That tension does not appear until you start doing interesting things.

Long Live The Silk Road

You see, there used to be a time when Bitcoin had not offended too many people. We were still in the "laughing at ourselves" stage, the ridicule stage of development. Then something interesting happened, called the Silk Road. How many people have heard of the Silk Road? All of you, very good. I won't ask. I am sure it was just insulin and asthma inhalers. *Audience laughs.*

The Silk Road brought Bitcoin to the limelight prematurely and scared off many potential bitcoiners. It generated a ton of bad publicity that haunts Bitcoin to this day. It associated the spending of money with the consumption of narcotics. Of course, if you want to malign a technology, talk of drugs is the first step, followed by child abuse, then terrorism is step three, but you might re-arrange them depending on your government's proclivities. If you want to stir up a nice big dollop of censorship, you will pick one of those three wrappings to deliver to the sheep, and tell them why it needs to be stopped.

I am no prude. When it comes to the consumption of narcotics and buying things in underground black markets, I understand. I think of drugs in terms of biology. Did you know that dolphins get high? You know about pufferfish, right? If you annoy them, they puff up and excrete a toxin on the surface of their skin. That toxin is annoying at least, and potentially fatal to most fish. Except for dolphins, who get high. Dolphins get high off of pufferfish poison. They will gather in a circle around a pufferfish, a dolphin will squeeze it in their mouth until it becomes annoyed and releases a bit of the toxin, and then they puff, puff, pass.

They understand the etiquette of puffer chewing. If we were the first species to not get high, that would be an anomaly in the animal kingdom. Evolutionary speaking, there are countless species of animals that get high or intoxicated.

When it comes to drug markets, I am a pragmatist. There is a reason people want to use online markets. The reason is really simple: you can't be stabbed over TCP/IP. It is all about reducing violence. Online markets have a very interesting effect on drugs. It immediately removes violence, which decreases the risk-based premium, brings prices down, and drives organized crime out of the market.

I will not try to persuade people that we should legalize this stuff here. Colorado is doing a pretty good job. But I do tell people that these things will continue to exist. This will keep happening because there has always been demand, and there will always be supply. Where demand and supply exist, markets will always emerge.

Right after the Silk Road emerged, the conversation around Bitcoin changed rapidly. Until then, quite a few large corporations were talking about becoming involved in it. They came up with this great phrase, "We are interested in the technology behind Bitcoin, the blockchain." That is the sound of ten thousand marketing officers backpedaling furiously, because they just read an article about Bitcoin and drug markets. "Oh shit. Take it off all the posters!"

And now I have news for you: "We are interested in the technology behind Ethereum: smart contracts." That is a phrase you will hear in the next few years, as people will start backpedaling furiously. The reason for that is, Ethereum could succeed in being a viable platform for writing unstoppable code. The next Silk Road could be fuelled by DAI, running on Swarm with Whisper communications, as a fully autonomous DApp, without administrators that you can give two life sentences plus forty years. It will be unstoppable.

When Ability Becomes Responsibility

The moment people figure this out, there will be calls to every prominent person, committee, foundation, authority, and governance body in Ethereum. Anyone who seems to have any control. They will say, "Yes, this is cute. But stop it. You have had your fun now. Yes, we heard about your unstoppable code, smart contracts, and DApps. Just stop it, okay? Now it has a drug market. You need to stop it now."

The smart people in Ethereum will say, "Well, I can't." The not-so-smart will say, "I won't."

Can't? Won't? What is the difference between can't and won't? **Two life sentences plus forty years is the difference between can't and won't.** When you say you want governance, beware what you ask for. Governance changes can't into won't. The moment you go over that line, what started as an ability becomes a responsibility. If you claim you don't have the ability anymore, that responsibility just became negligence. Criminal negligence.

Governance and unstoppable code will form this very fine line that we must tread carefully. Is your line the Silk Road? Probably not. I mean, look where we are. Look at this crowd. What about child porn or terrorism financing?

The Relativity of Legality and Morality

Here is the problem: we all have a moral compass. We all have a set of principles and ideals that we would like to believe are universal, that we all believe in one code of conduct. Where do you source yours? Maybe from a book, evolution, parenting, or socialization. Maybe from Montessori. I don't know, but you acquired it somehow. You have a moral code.

Well, I have bad news for you. It is not universal. It is highly subjective and incredibly relative. Let's talk about moral relativism, which is a fun topic especially for conservatives. I am a moral relativist, not because I believe that moral relativism is the moral choice. Ironically, it isn't. Moral relativism is the pragmatic recognition that, when I look around me, read my history books, and look at other cultures or religions, people with other capabilities and chances than I had, they don't share my morality. I am hard-pressed to find any two people who share everything in their moral code.

This is where the crux of governance versus unstoppable code comes to a head. In every conversation I hear about governance among affluent, privileged northern American or western European people who share 90% of a common morality code — but only represent 15% of the human population — I am wondering, what are you thinking when you say that governance must be subservient to a legal framework? That we need an anchor based in law? Whose law? Maybe you assume your law. I wouldn't assume that.

Every time someone says, "That is illegal," your response shouldn't be, "Oh, right." Your response should be to ask, "Where? Illegal where?" If you understand one thing about the law, you know that 'where' is the most important question. In Denver? In Colorado? In Wyoming or South Dakota? If you leave Colorado after using marijuana, and go to South Carolina, they can arrest you for possession, for the trace amounts in your bloodstream. They don't share Colorado's laws. You don't need to go very far to cross that line. You may not even know that you crossed that line, but the law suddenly changed very radically. And that's just in this country.

If you go a bit further out, things become really weird. We live in a bubble. We assume that our morality is the one true doctrine, ethos, and culture. "USA!" But the truth is, we live in a varied world. When you talk about governance and applying the law, the fundamental problem is where, and whose law. And oh will you will hate some of those laws.

Atheism is illegal and punishable by death in more than ten countries. Not ideas or actions. Just the failure to believe in one or more gods, is illegal. Even if the person says nothing about their beliefs, or non-beliefs, their mere existence is illegal. According to the law, they deserve to die. It's illegal to identify, or even simply be, LGBTQ in eighty-three countries. In North Korea, only six hairstyles are allowed for men. *Andreas points to his own hairstyle.* It's clear my existence there is illegal. You may have noticed that I managed to call this a "hairstyle," as if I have a choice in a receding hairline. Denial! *Audience laughs.*

The point is, the morality and laws that you apply will be highly relative. If you set up a system of unstoppable code that is globally accessible and borderless from day one, you will need to contend with two possible scenarios: either no laws or all laws apply. The second option is impossible. You cannot comply with all laws. There will be contradictions. In some jurisdictions, what you are doing is illegal. I will just go for *no laws*. Fuck it. Unstoppable code. No permission, no apologies, no reservations.

The Power of Unstoppable Code

Think about this for a principle: for every bad application for unstoppable code, I can think of one hundred good applications. Though they will seem abhorrent to countries that do not share my moral code, such as self sovereignty for women in Saudi Arabia. A DApp that helps thirteen-year-old brides to escape the hell-hole of their impending marriage would be abhorrent to their culture. You could insert four or five countries here, where that is abhorrent in their culture. It would be moral in my view, but it is not my view that matters.

If you create a framework for unstoppable code, what applications can we write as human beings? What applications will we write as human beings? I think we will write some great applications. While we don't share morality, one of the common themes of humanity is goodness. We all share that. The vast majority of people, given unstoppable code, will create applications that enable them to give their family a future, their children an education, health care, sanitation, housing, and opportunity. That is what people do with freedom.

Guess what? Freedom itself is abhorrent in dozens of places around the world. Unstoppable code can fix that. But if you apply governance to override, overrule, backtrack, remove, and reverse, you will have the ability and then the responsibility. You will be asked wherever your code appears, which is in every jurisdiction, to exercise that ability.

The *Oops* Clause: A Double-Edged Sword

Maybe you can say, "No," because they can't reach you. But they will reach you somehow. You live in at least one country. You never know, we might screw up an election, and then our own government is "asking" us to do abhorrent things. What will you do then?

Governance is a double-edged sword. With the DApps we have today, in many cases we need to have an oops clause. Oops, I locked $150 million in my multi-signature wallet system! Oops, my decentralized autonomous mutual fund just blew up! Okay, we may need some forms of governance. But be careful when you put those in. Think carefully about what capabilities you want to give to whom.

If you do put in an oops clause, make it an oops clause that blows up the entire DApp, preferably so you can fix that problem and start a new one with less of an oops clause. Don't put an oops clause that allows you to reverse only one transaction or narrowly tailor an intervention.

There is a principle in United States law, which is the idea of a common carrier. A common carrier is like a service provider or platform that does not create or post content; therefore, they have a degree of immunity from responsibility for the content posted or transmitted across their platform by users.

If I use a phone and arrange a conspiracy to commit a crime, AT&T is not responsible for stopping me. They cannot be held liable. They cannot and will not tailor responses to specific content. If they were picking and choosing, exercising discretion and moderating, if they demonstrate the ability to remove some content, then the requests will pour in.

I've been in some of these offices and seen it happen. There is a fax machine in the corner. Every few minutes, it spits out the page, with an eagle holding a sword and shield at the top, that says, "Sheriff of Piss-Ville Podunk Little Town compels you to do this." If you open yourself to that, you will soon learn the names of some very exotic places, followed by the words cease and desist.

So don't. Don't allow content-based restrictions. Don't build systems where you have moderating ability. Don't give yourself the power to stop unstoppable code. Embrace the fact that what we are doing is important.

We Already Have Stoppable Code

It will require courage. Before long, we will hear some very different sounds from the Enterprise Alliance, the corporate partners, senior executives and board dudes, the consultants and the MBAs. We need to remember why we are doing this, why we are building this. Because there is no point in building stoppable code. We already have that. It is called the cloud, an international surveillance engine. You put your data on other people's computers, so they can steal your privacy every day and make billions of dollars. We already have stoppable code.

And if we will build more stoppable code, for god's sake — don't do it on infrastructure that is so hard to scale, so bloody inefficient, that just explaining the most basic concepts takes 420 pages and two years of my life! *Audience laughs.*

If you need more stoppable code, I'd suggest Microsoft SQL Server Enterprise Edition, with a replication engine. Got it? That is the platform for stoppable code. Centralized databases. We have them already. They work, they're efficient, we know how to use them. There are thousands, if not millions, of people trained on them. We don't need that platform.

This platform is for unstoppable code. This platform is our promise to the future. We will do things differently, because it matters.

Thank you.

Picking the Right Blockchain for the Job

The original video presentation of this talk was recorded at the *DigitalK Conference* in Sofia, Bulgaria; May 2019. Video Link: https://aantonop.io/PickingBlockchains

The Best Blockchain

Today, I want to talk to you about which blockchain is the "best" blockchain. Are you ready? Let's ask the audience. Altogether, at the count of three, you shout out which blockchain you think is the best. Three, two, one…

I hear: Bitcoin! Ethereum! Litecoin! Fantastic.

That is what subjective experience is all about. We all have opinions, but opinions really don't matter. It doesn't matter if it is the best blockchain in your opinion or not. Maybe it does matter if you are a trader, and you need to guess what everybody else thinks it is. The point is, it is all about perception.

I am not going to tell you which blockchain is the best. I think that is a ridiculous question to even ask. It is a bit like asking, "What is the best car?" "What is the best pair of shoes?" It depends on what you want to achieve with this car or pair of shoes. If you ask someone what the best pair of shoes is, they may tell you: strong hiking boots. If you ask someone else, they may tell you: Manolo Blahniks. Have you ever tried hiking in Manolo Blahniks? Have you ever walked a fashion show in hiking boots? They wouldn't work so well, right? Purpose matters. The purpose you want to build the tool for matters. The purpose determines what the best blockchain will be.

The general question, "what is the best blockchain?, makes no sense. You need to state the purpose. You can ask, "What is the best blockchain for my purpose?" "What is the best cryptocurrency for my purpose?" But you can't just ask, "what is the best?" That makes no sense.

If you start reading the marketing brochures, I'm sure they will contradict what I just said. They will tell you, "This blockchain can do everything. It is scalable, secure, and fast." "It does smart contracts and sound money." "It is quantum resistant, super private, and uses military-grade encryption." That last part just means 128-bit encryption and it's bullshit, which is the purpose of a marketing brochure, of course. People will make a lot of promises about their favorite project, but you should really ask what the purpose is. What are you trying to achieve?

Form Should Follow Function

In architecture, there is a great phrase from the 1980s, which is: form follows function. The idea is, with any building, the way it looks should communicate what it is used for. The form should follow the function; the architecture of the building should reflect the purpose. The same thing applies to blockchains. The architecture of the system should reflect what it is intended to be used for. But that is a very difficult thing to do, for architects, software engineers, and product managers. It is even more difficult in open-source, public blockchains. They are the only ones I care about and think are interesting.

It is difficult to wade through all of the opinions about what a blockchain might do or will do. Pick any one of the open public blockchains that exists today, and ask twenty developers working on it about what the primary purpose is. What is this thing supposed to do? They will give you twenty different answers. "Sound money." "Digital cash." "It can handle smart contracts." "It can do everything you need." But what does it do for you? That is a more interesting question. You must decide what fits the application you are trying to build.

You Don't Need a Blockchain For That

Unfortunately, that question is not asked a lot. You can tell, because people are still trying to apply blockchain technology to a whole bunch of things that don't need a blockchain. I have considered wearing a t-shirt at all blockchain conferences which says, "You don't need a blockchain for that." Recently I was a judge in a hackathon event and one of the teams proudly announced, "We have put digital music on the blockchain." All I could think was "You don't need a blockchain for that." So I asked, "Why would you need a blockchain for that?" They weren't able to answer it.

What does a blockchain do? It is not a content database. It is not just somewhere you record digital signatures. You certainly don't need a blockchain for just that. It is not scalable or efficient. It is decentralized, secure, and (for the ones I care about) very robust against censorship. That means it should keep running even when very powerful people or organizations want to stop it from running. For that use case, you need a blockchain.

But what kind of blockchain? How would you design it?

Intractable Trade-offs

Let's talk about the engineering challenges when building these systems. You need to make choices. Some of these choices come up at a very early stage. For example, do I want to build a system that is very specific, or with a broad generic purpose? Why don't we just do both? You can't do both. Systems that are specific need to be optimised for that purpose. In doing so, they are no longer flexible enough to handle the general purpose. Systems that are general-purpose don't have the unique characteristics you need for specific applications. That should be a conscious decision at the beginning. Some blockchains are designed for rather specific applications; some blockchains are designed to handle generic applications. Both often claim that they can be both.

Once you have made a decision on that first question, you need to make further decisions, all of which involve more intractable trade-offs. "Intractable" means you can't get both sides. I must choose one or the other. That choice then determines the path that the blockchain will take.

As a developer, designer, or architect, you don't have the power to tell the market how they will use your product. If you try to be too specific, the market may decide that it is not suitable for what they need. If you try to be too generic, but you only have one type of application in mind, the market may decide to use it for a completely different type of application. Hopefully, they will.

As a developer, designer, or architect, you rarely have the exclusive knowledge of what other people need. There is too much variety. You can barely imagine what people might need in other places in the world that you don't understand, under different circumstances than your own. You certainly can't do that across a broad time-frame.

We are building systems that might last, should last, will last, for decades. What do people need today? What will people need in 30 years? Very different answers. The developers who are making these very careful trade-offs, need to consider that they are making those decisions with incomplete information. Even if they try to design something with very specific applications in mind, the market may decide to do something completely different.

Another Function May Fit the Form

Back to architecture history. In the 1960s and 1970s, in California, they made swimming pools in organic shapes. No longer square, but with curves. Have you seen those types of swimming pools? Then there was a big drought; for a couple years, it was forbidden to fill your swimming pool because there wasn't enough water.

Guess what happened next? Skateboarding exploded in popularity across California. Skateboarders saw those curves and thought, *If I stand on the edge and kick down, we could have some fun with this!* All of the swimming pools which had been designed with curves, became the first skate parks. Skateboarding wasn't a big deal before then and mostly involved riding in straight, flat lines. That sport was transformed.

Do you think the swimming pool designers could imagine that, ten years later, some snotty nosed kid would go whizzing around them on wheels? No. Form follows function... sometimes. Sometimes, it doesn't. Sometimes the form follows the function that the designer thought it would have, and then the market says, "I have another function that fits perfectly with this curve." You can never know how that will play out.

Users Decide Function

The same thing will happen with blockchains. Ultimately, the users and the market decide. You can have all the ideas you want, you can even have a panel of six very serious experts. Some of them will say, "It is a store-of-value." Somebody else will say, "It is a medium-of-exchange." Another one will say, "It can't be a unit-of-account, because the volatility is too high." And then someone will say, "Maybe we should focus on smart contracts." But they don't really know what they're talking about, because they don't get to decide for everyone. These are opinions, but they don't represent every user. Users will decide.

You can make something that seems to fit better with a store-of-value use case, or a smart contracts use case. The developers and designers of Bitcoin had some ideas about it being digital cash. For some period of time, it plays as digital cash. For another period of time, it plays as speculative gambling money. And in other times, it plays as a store-of-value, especially in countries where their currency is distressed. Which of those will it be? We don't know.

It depends on a lot of factors that we don't know yet. It depends on what happens to national currencies and inflation in the U.S., Europe, and Japan. It depends on how the world transforms. It depends on whether cash, as it exists today, will still exist in fifteen years. All of these factors have nothing to do with bitcoin.

The designers of Ethereum had certain applications in mind, mostly engineering applications. Did they think it would become a platform for launching ten thousand scams and pump-and-dumps? No, but it was very good at that! A generic, flexible platform to build whatever smart contract you can imagine, will attract the kind of person who wants to build a beautifully engineered pump-and-dump scheme. Does that change what Ethereum does as a whole? No. It just means, it was a niche that the market decided was really hot. Why? Because a whole bunch of naive investors, and even more naive venture capitalists, were throwing as much money as possible into this new space.

You Don't Need a Blockchain For That Either

Two years ago, you could attach "blockchain" to any other word, and a venture capitalist would throw a couple million dollars at you. Music? Blockchain. Movies? Blockchain! Real-estate? Blockchain. Asparagus? Blockchain asparagus. "Two million dollars for you, sir. That sounds fascinating."

You could even combine it with the other *cool* words. "We will cultivate asparagus with blockchain-based, artificial intelligence directed autonomous drones." That way, you could check all of the boxes, and they would throw tens of millions of dollars at you. None of it made any sense! The market not only decides, but sometimes the market is stupid, bizarre, and irrational. It is driven by sentiment and emotion.

Over the next decade, things will calm down. People will figure out that you don't need a blockchain for that. How will most of them figure that out? They will invest their money and then lose their money. They will invest more of their money and then lose it again. By the third loss, most smart investors would start picking up on that pattern. For the less smart investors, it may take them ten or fifteen rounds of losses.

The bottom line is, there is no "best" for every purpose. The people involved in making difficult trade-offs every day, cannot design for a purpose that is too specific. That can be limiting and miss what the market may want to do. They can miss the timing. They also can't design something that is too generic, because it won't have enough powerful capabilities to solve real problems that we have. They will need to make difficult trade-offs. You can't simply be scalable, decentralized, secure, and fast at the same time.

A Blockchain Trilemma

In engineering terms, there are some fundamental trade-offs. We categorize them as dilemmas or trilemmas. A classic trilemma is: security, decentralization, and scalability. In a trilemma, you can only pick two of the three options. If you make something that is maximally scalable and secure, it probably won't be very decentralized. If you make something that is maximally scalable and decentralized, it probably won't be secure. If you make something that is maximally decentralized and secure, it probably won't be very scalable.

Of course, there will be blockchain projects that tell you, "We can do all three!" That means they don't understand the trade-off, which is even more dangerous. There are two possibilities: lying or ignorance. Ignorance of the trilemma is far worse.

This is what I used to tell my consultation clients: "I can deliver the solution fast, cheap, or great. Pick two. I can do it fast and cheap, but it won't be the best. I can do it cheap and it will be great, but it won't be fast. I can do it fast and it will be great, but trust me, it won't be cheap!" That is the essence of a trilemma we face every day in life.

Life involves choices. Think of it as a journey. When you go through the door on the left, you may lose whatever is through the right door. You may never be able to go back and take that road, and the roads that branch off from it. You have made your choice.

When dealing with building the best blockchain for a specific purpose, every choice you make, whether you know it or not, can close as many possibilities as it opens. The next time someone asks you, "What is the best blockchain," instead of shouting out the name of your favorite, ask "For what?"

Thank you very much!

Keeping Digital Communities Weird

The original video presentation of this talk was recorded at the *Polish Bitcoin Congress (Polski Kongres Bitcoin)* in Warsaw, Poland; May 2018. Video Link: https://aantonop.io/KeepingWeird

I want to talk today about communities; how we build interesting, exciting communities, both online and in person.

Cool Neighborhoods Don't Last

I've traveled a lot in my life. I've lived in many, many different places. I find that I am always attracted to a certain kind of neighborhood. I like to live in a place where there are a lot of artists, a lot of musicians. I like to live in neighborhoods that have weird little coffee shops and obscure bars where people play live music. I like neighborhoods where you get to see graffiti on the walls. Perhaps places that — at least when I live in those places — are not that safe. You know? They're still a bit dangerous.

But those neighborhoods don't last. The artists, the musicians, the poor students, the people who are living in those neighborhoods, love those neighborhoods too because rent is cheap. The development of the neighborhood hasn't happened yet and there are opportunities for expression. Many weird and creative people live in those neighborhoods.

Inevitably, when you stay in a neighborhood like that long enough, other people notice. It starts becoming a "cool" neighborhood. When it becomes a cool neighborhood, people who could afford a higher rent start moving into that neighborhood. Then richer and richer people start moving into that neighborhood. In a year or two, there's a Starbucks on the corner. The interesting bar that had all of the weird and quirky musicians is replaced by a gallery or boutique that sells a bit more upscale, more expensive clothes than before.

Then the rents start going up, the real estate property values start going up. Before long, the artists, musicians, and the interesting people who are the reason you moved to that neighborhood, can't afford to live there anymore. So they move and eventually the neighborhood is full of young professionals wearing suits, going to work every morning, 9am to 5pm.

With their Starbucks coffee in their hand. They're very busy and they're on their phone. That neighborhood is now shit. It's not a cool neighborhood anymore, so you have to start looking for the next cool neighborhood. The cycle repeats.

Gentrification is the word we use in the United States to describe that phenomenon. Turns out that all of the things that make a neighborhood interesting, all of the quirky and weird people, they don't stay very long. If you like to live in that environment, an environment that is full of creativity and expression, the worst things that can happen are commodification, corporatization, marketing.

If you take something that is cool and authentic, and you turn it into a marketing campaign for Coca-Cola or Nike, it's not cool anymore. By the time they think it's cool, it's not cool anymore. It ruins the authenticity. The money starts pouring in and all of the authenticity is gone.

The First Digital Communities

I first went online and participated in digital communities in the 1980s. In order to participate in those digital communities, I had to buy a modem. I had to dial into a bulletin board system. This bulletin board system was run by some person in their basement as a hobby. It had maybe a hundred and fifty participants in it, who were all just as weird as I was. Weird teenage kids with modems, who other people didn't understand. We had such a good time having conversations online.

Then towards the end of the 80s, bulletin board systems (BBSs) started getting popular. Big companies started buying the smaller operators, advertising, charging membership fees, "polishing" and "improving" the content. They tried to make it a bit more palatable for mainstream. "Watch your language." "Don't say bad words." "Only things for adults." "Let's keep this family-friendly." All of the interesting and weird people who made the bulletin board system interesting in the first place started looking for somewhere else to have their conversations, because they weren't welcome anymore. In some cases, because they can't afford to participate anymore. All of the creative conversation, the reason we went there in the first place, is now gone.

In fact, one of the weird things about these bulletin board systems in those days... it was mostly guys. There were almost no women participating in online bulletin board systems in 1985. But the corporations tried to convert these bulletin board systems into dating sites. They had guys pretend to be women so they could attract more customers. You could find yourself in a situation, having a conversation with another guy whose online name is "Helen," in order to sell more subscriptions to the bulletin board system. Marketing!

The funny thing: there were a few women online at that time and they were using guys' names so they could feel more comfortable and less freaked out by weirdos. They had the fake "Helen" talking to them, fake flirting to try to get them to pay more for a subscription.

By that time, I had already moved on to Usenet. Usenet was a group discussion that was happening across all of the Internet at the time, towards the end of the 1980s. It was a text-based community where you could exchange messages with anyone around the world who was on the internet. At the time, that was maybe 500,000 people.

Usenet was weird, very weird in fact. There was a special corner of Usenet called the alt groups, the alternative groups, that you couldn't access in all places. But where you could access them, that was the special place. That's where all of the Dungeons & Dragons fans, all the comic book fans, all the weird sci-fi fans, a lot of the sex and other weird hobbies met. Generally, people who didn't fit well into other groups were in the alt groups.

The Gentrification of the Web

Then the corporations came. They started carrying Usenet as a subscription service. The first thing they dropped was the alt groups. Now you could pay to get the clean version of Usenet, but you couldn't get the alt groups because those weren't very polite at times. They weren't very corporate. They weren't very clean. They took Usenet with all of its weirdness, all of its quirkiness, and they dressed it in a suit, cut its hair, and it became boring. All of the interesting people moved on.

Then the Web happened. With the web we had this explosion of creativity and expression. At first, all of the websites were weird: too many colors, blinking tags and fonts, everything looked terrible. There was no sense of design. But the conversations you could have, the creativity and the weird people you could meet, were fantastic.

Then the corporations came in again. They polished everything and cleaned it up. "No bad words on this site!" "This is moderated content." CompuServe and AOL came along, and they built curated environments protected from all the dirty words and all the weird people. Gentrification came in waves across the internet, and our digital domain was being gentrified just like a neighborhood. With every cycle of gentrification, it is the same result: the people who went there who made that place interesting were no longer welcome, couldn't afford to participate, not allowed to speak. And so they leave. All of the reasons why you joined in the first place are no longer there. Many of the people who left all of those curated environments went to other parts of the Web, started their own websites and independent communities.

Then Web 2.0 happened. When Web 2.0 happened, we got the MySpaces, then the Facebooks and other social media sites. They very carefully curate the content. You can post Nazi messages on Facebook and get away with it for a while, but God help you if you show a breast. Oh, no, we can't have that. It's a family environment. Don't say bad words. Carefully curated, lots of marketing, very polished. All of the interesting people leave.

If you still have a Facebook account, it's so you can see photos of your grandchildren. Kids don't want to be on Facebook. The reason they don't want to be on Facebook is because their parents are there now. And so they leave. They go to Reddit and 4chan. Gentrification...

Bitcoin, Blockchain, and Bullshit, Oh My!

Bitcoin was weird. I really loved Bitcoin when it was weird. But for some people, Bitcoin was too weird, too difficult to understand. There was a small possibility that you could buy drugs with bitcoin. But not the good drugs. Not the drugs made by Pfizer that cost a lot of money. Not Adderall, which is an amphetamine. Not Fentanyl, which is heroin. Not prescription good drugs. Bad drugs. Like marijuana. People could buy drugs. They could do other things that were not very good for the corporate image.

So how do you gentrify a currency? How do you take something that is weird, dress it up in a suit, give it a haircut, present it to board executives? I remember the first few years when companies would ask me to give talks at their headquarters. They would say, "We want you to talk to our executives, but when you talk to them, could you please say *blockchain*? Don't say *Bitcoin*, because Bitcoin is weird and blockchain is the future."

And I said, "No, I won't say *blockchain*. I will say *Bitcoin*, because Bitcoin is the future and blockchain is bullshit. I'll also say *bullshit* to your executives, because you paid me to come here and tell you the truth as I see it. I'm not going to try to sell you something that's nicely packaged, just to avoid offending. I'm interested in telling the truth."

The reason cryptocurrencies are interesting, the reason Bitcoin is interesting, is because it's not controlled. It can't be censored, because it's open. A lot of the people involved are very "weird." Weird computer geeks, weird cryptographers who have weird ideas about privacy and freedom. These weird people are why I'm involved in Bitcoin, because I'm weird too and that's okay. If you take all of that out, what you're left with — this blockchain — is a sterile, inexpressive, un-innovative environment. A corporate plaything that has been sanitized of everything interesting and left as an empty shell. It's basically a very slow database.

If someone comes to you and asks, "Do I need a blockchain for my business," ask them: "Do you need something that is open, neutral, borderless, which no one controls and resists censorship?" If yes, then you need Bitcoin. Or Ethereum. Monero. Zcash. Some open, public, blockchain cryptocurrency system that expresses these capabilities.

But if you don't need something that's open, borderless, neutral, censorship-resistant, and not controlled by anyone, what you're really asking for is a database. So install a database. You don't need a blockchain. If you're just trying to do is business-as-usual, but now with a blockchain, you really want a database. If the purpose of introducing this technology into your bank is to be able to not change anything about how you do business, then you're looking for a database. Or if your government says, "We will do a digital currency. We heard there's a digital currency using *blockchain* that is open, decentralized, borderless, censorship-resistant, and neutral. Except we don't want it to be open, decentralized, censorship-resistant, neutral or borderless. We want it to be controlled within our borders, with the ability to control who has access to it, with full censorship. We ultimately decide who has power on this system." Guess what? That is also known as a database. You can build that and it will be boring.

All of the innovation, all of the excitement, all the reasons why I'm interested in these technologies — and perhaps why some of you are — is precisely because they're weird, different, and open. Because they allow everyone to innovate and express themselves creatively in ways that we don't anticipate. In ways that are completely unpredictable and, in some ways, that are offensive. That's okay.

I don't want to live in a world of pastel colors, carefully curated advertising, marketing-focused tested phrases, where you can't say the bad words. I want to live in a world with color, with creativity, with variety, with diversity, with ideas. Ideas that sometimes offend me and scare me, that I don't understand, with weird people around me who are free to express themselves, because that's where creativity comes from.

It is not just Bitcoin. We will see this happen again and again. We've already gone through the phase where people said, "Yes, I'm interested in blockchain, but not Bitcoin." When someone tells you, "I'm interested in blockchain but not Bitcoin," what they mean is "I don't understand." Or they've heard someone else say it and they think they can be cool if they say that too. It's a bit like someone saying, "MySpace is so last year. I'm into Facebook now." It happened to Bitcoin, but it's going to keep happening. It's going to keep happening to every cryptocurrency that dares to do something interesting.

Fork Off

Right now, the big banks and governments, they're in love with Ethereum. They love the fact that Ethereum has all of these capabilities that seem much less weird than Bitcoin. But they don't realize: all of the weirdness is still there. I love the weirdness in Ethereum because, quite honestly, the whole point of Ethereum is to make unstoppable code, applications that you cannot turn off. The reason you can't turn them off is because they're decentralized apps, DApps. Why make a DApp unless you want to make a DApp that somebody wants to turn off, and you want to continue working? The whole point of an uncensorable application is writing applications that are offensive to some people.

At some point in the next couple of years, someone is going to write a weird application on Ethereum. The big banks and all of the organizations that today are absolutely enamored with Ethereum will go running to

the Ethereum Foundation and to the Ethereum Enterprise Alliance.
They're going to say, "Hey, we'd like you to stop this." And the Ethereum
Foundation is going to say, most likely, "No, we won't." Or better yet, "We
can't." "Submit your Ethereum Improvement Proposal. Let's see what the
community thinks. Hey, community. Do you want to stop this application?
Because JP Morgan Chase doesn't like it. No? Oops."

Or maybe they decide to stop it and we get another hard fork. Then we have
three Ethereums. Ethereum, Ethereum Classic, and Ethereum Uncensored.
Because you can't stop these things. All you can do is fork away a bullshit
corporate version. But the other one continues to run. Then what do you
have?

We Can't Be Gentrified

That's the moment you suddenly realize: this is the first time we have a
digital community that can't be gentrified. You can plant your Starbucks
on the corner, but you can't kick out the weirdos. If you try to kick out the
weirdos, we fork it and we take the neighborhood with us. The weirdos own
this neighborhood for the first time ever and they can't be kicked out. That's
beautiful. That's what this is all about. For the first time, we now have
digital communities that can't be taken over, polished, sanitized, sterilized
of any idea worthwhile and turned into a plaything for Disney, McDonald's,
Coca-Cola, JPMorgan Chase to shit all over the creativity and turn it into
empty marketing slogans.

For the first time, we have digital communities that can't be gentrified.
When people ask me, "Why are you excited about cryptocurrencies? Aren't
they weird?" I say, "Yes! They're weird; they're beautifully weird. That's
why I'm interested in them." My pledge, and the pledge of all the other
people who are in this because it's weird, is to keep it weird.

Thank you.

Crypto-Winter to the North, Crypto-Summer to the South

The original video presentation of this talk was recorded at the *Bitcoin Argentina Meetup in Collaboration with the Bitcoin Embassy* in Buenos Aires, Argentina; January 2019. Video Link: https://aantonop.io/CryptoWinter

Oh my god, everyone came! Three months ago, I gave a talk in Seattle, a big theater with seven hundred seats. I was optimistic, because I have had big audiences before. *It is Seattle, of course they will come.* Microsoft, Amazon, all these tech companies are there. But in eight weeks, we did not even sell three hundred tickets. Because in Seattle, it is crypto-winter. Not just winter, crypto-winter. A lot of the people who became very excited in October 2017, for mysterious reasons, became very unexcited in March 2018 for equally mysterious reasons.

But not here. Here in Buenos Aires it is crypto-summer. All seats sold out in five days! Give a big round of applause to Rodolfo and more than twenty volunteers who came together to help me make this happen. Thank you so much to all of those who supported and worked really hard to make this event possible. Of course, to the sponsors as well. All of the work we do tonight will go towards charity.

The Seasons of Crypto

Let's start with these concepts of crypto-winter and crypto-summer. How many seasonal variations of the volatile cryptocurrency markets have you been through so far? How many people have been through four bubble cycles? A couple of hands. Three bubble cycles? Two bubble cycles? And newbies, one bubble cycle? Don't worry - there is another one coming!

In crypto-markets, like any new technology, there are these waves of enthusiasm and speculation. Then people forget and move away. They come back later with the next cycle. Why? Because most of the people getting involved today don't actually need it. They only use crypto because it is something to speculate in. They are not interested in the potential of what cryptocurrency can do for their lives today, but in the potential of its value increasing due to how it affects the life of somebody else, at some other time.

That is not the attitude in Argentina, South America, Southeast Asia, or South Africa. In those places, the value of cryptocurrency isn't about something that happens later. It is not about, *if my government suddenly became corrupt, if my bank started stealing our pensions, if our speech was censored, our associations restricted, and our political parties imprisoned... if, if if...* But it's not an "if" in those places. These things are already happening there.

Americans have a hard time understanding this. They have the privilege and luxury of stability, but their circumstances are exceptional. In much of the world, corrupt governments and banks are raiding pension funds and imprisoning the opposition. There are cancelled elections and elections with a 96% majority vote. Those things happen all across the world. That is the average human experience. That is the reason why crypto is so important. They are systems that allow us to find new, 21st century ways of organizing societal institutions, instead of 19th century ways that have failed to scale.

What Does Success Look Like?

When we have this explosion of interest in cryptocurrencies, many of us find ourselves talking to people who seem to be speaking a different language. They are very interested in the price and which shitcoin will be the *next big thing*. They are very interested in understanding how they can *fake it until they make it* to be successful.

When I am asked to talk to companies about cryptocurrencies and blockchains, and they tell me about their "wonderful new project," I ask them, "What is success to you? Let's say that you succeed. What does your company achieve? Describe success to me." Inevitably, they fail to answer that question. In many cases, they haven't actually thought about what success will look like, other than, "We will make loads of money!"

This is a very important question to ask: **what does success look like to you?** "We will build the best product that dominates the market and make us lots of money!" Who does that help? "Me." Okay, great. But that is not enough people. Can we think about how we can help more people? Your current business plan is about helping four people. Can we increase the scale a bit? Can we think about helping more people?

When the markets surge this space is suddenly flooded by outsiders, opportunistic people who arrive because they read an article in The Wall Street Journal or the magazine in the seat pocket of their flight, or because their colleagues are telling them: "This will be the next big thing like AI and quantum computing!" They come to this space and bring a set of assumptions with them.

The Zero-Sum Game

One of the assumptions is what I want to talk about today, and that's the assumption that markets operate as a zero-sum game. They won't tell you this because sometimes they don't even know that is what they are thinking. It is a very important assumption. You must be very careful to notice it. When you have a business discussion, when you are talking to your friends about the latest crypto project they are interested in, the implication under many of these conversations is the concept of a zero-sum game.

A zero-sum game is an environment in which one party wins only if the other party loses. It is not a situation where both parties win, or where everybody wins. In a zero-sum game, you win at the expense of others.

This is a toxic assumption that exists in every cycle of business. It is pretty much what earning an MBA is about, teaching you how to play the zero-sum games and crush your competition. It is not about making a better world, a better product, a better market, or increasing competition. It is about finding out what the rules are, figuring out how to exploit those rules, and building a fence around your intellectual property, your products, and your market niche. It's about learning how to prevent anyone from competing with you; learning how to capture customers- not acquire, *capture* customers, herd them into this fenced area, and extract as much money as you can. That's modern business in a nutshell.

This toxic assumption in every cycle of business stems from some important considerations. The most important factor is the absence of free markets. In a free market, you don't play a zero-sum game and you can't stop competitors from entering. In a free market, if you create something new, others will emerge to build on it and also bring new customers, new opportunities, and market niches so that everyone can enjoy it and win. In free markets, it is not a zero-sum game.

So then where is this idea coming from? It comes from the fact that most of the celebrated capitalists in the world have never seen a free market in their entire lives! They operate in an environment where they come to own the regulators and write the rules. Their primary goal is to cheat enough to ensure that no one can stop them from acquiring the holy grail of business: a monopoly. Once you have a monopoly, you can work to prevent anyone from breaking into it, and extract as much value as you can from your customers. It is not about competition, improving markets or the world. It is about establishing monopolies. They bring that attitude into the crypto space and start spreading it like a poison in every business.

Rules Without Rulers

If you pay attention you'll see these assumptions all around you. "We cannot open-source our wallet! If we open-source it, our competitors will copy it." "We need to find out who the regulators are. In fact, we should invite them to regulate our industry. Then we will know what the rules are."

What else do you need to know about the rules? The rules are pretty simple: one block every ten minutes and twenty-one million coins. They seem like pretty simple rules. We know what the rules are. They are enforced by network consensus. The smart contract will execute, the token will be issued under these conditions. The rules are clear. Why do you need different rules?

"Oh, because we can't fix those rules to benefit us. But we can fix the human rules with lobbying. We want to unleash our NDAs (non-disclosure agreements) in the market. We want to round up all possible customers and create a nice cozy monopoly, a zero-sum game."

The maximialists think, "Our crypto cannot win unless their crypto loses!" If that's the case, it becomes very important to point out all the ways the other crypto project is not pure enough, how it is not the original vision of the founder, how it is not innovating in the correct direction. That is the zero-sum thinking infecting our industry.

In an open-source industry like ours, it doesn't hurt you if another cryptocurrency builds something good. Copy it. It is open-source. Learn more about it. This is a beautiful environment where every invention made anywhere in the entire ecosystem becomes one that everyone can use.

It is not just the successes that are valuable. Every failure is also a lesson, a lesson someone else learned the hard way so that you don't need to. In business, even more valuable than a success, is a failure that didn't cost you anything to learn.

Our Creative Commons

Our environment has a different set of rules. We are not suffering from the tragedy of the commons. We have a creative commons. The open-source culture is not just technological, it's not just our computer code. It is an open culture of creative people, which has all arrived at this singular moment in history and agreed to one fundamental premise: this might be a better way. These people are already on our side of the fence. The other side of the fence is a zero-sum game, with the corrupt governments, banks, and monopoly systems that create massive inequality, economic failure, and wasted talent all around the world.

Shitcoins...

So if your friend has finally crossed over to this side, with the idea that there might be something better, and there might be a new way of doing things, what will you do? Will you turn to them and say, "You bought what? *That* is a shitcoin, you heretic!" No! You should say, "Welcome, my friend. Buy shitcoins if you want. But while you're here, maybe, instead of just buying, I can teach you about the technology. You could learn about what you can do with it and how to apply it in your own life. You will learn some skills and be able to use them in a business. You can explore lots of possibilities, and not just treat this as an investment. Also, you probably shouldn't buy that shitcoin. Really, don't. But welcome to crypto!"

Even if you were the "friend" who bought shitcoins, you have still made the very important mental leap in figuring out that we are trying to build something different, something new. You are already part of our creative commons. And I welcome you. I will welcome everybody who comes in, for whatever reason, good or bad. It doesn't matter, as long as they are not bringing this zero-sum mentality, that we can only succeed if somebody else fails. We don't do that in open-source industries. We don't do that in free markets. We don't do that here. We have a creative commons that doesn't cause a tragedy of the commons, where everyone exploits the resources, fences them off, and sucks them dry until there is nothing left.

Sharing Knowledge

In a creative commons, everything is shared. If I consume from your knowledge, you will not lose that knowledge. You will have it and so will everybody else. If someone downloads my book without buying it, I didn't lose a book because they didn't buy it, but I have gained a reader who gave me one of the most important things in life: attention. They had the ability to sit down and breathe for just a second, to push aside the noise and read something. If somebody reads my book, I am thankful for their time. Maybe they won't even make it past chapter one. That is okay.

When I met with my first publisher O'Reilly Media and said, "I will publish this book under an open-source license. It will be free to read and to share. For the first year, no one will be allowed to commercialize it. After the first year, it will be free to translate and re-sell by everyone in the world. You can use it to make a musical performance if you want to." (You don't want to.) They were reluctant, they were understandably concerned about how they would make money. But that is not what I am here for. That is not what this is about.

The real question is "How will we change the world?" How will we bring something new, different, and creative into the world? If you do that, don't worry. People will appreciate it. They will find a way to reward you. If you are lucky, they will give you money. If you are really lucky, they will give you passion, creativity, and commitment. They will change their minds. They will go out and change the minds of other people. That reward is a hell of a lot more powerful. That is what we build hope on.

Built By Professionals

When the market is booming, in come the zero-sum gamers. They say, "In order to really grow, we need investors." But investors have expectations. They ask, "Where is the intellectual property that we can build a fence around? Where is the product that will prevent competitors from entering the market? How do we win by crushing everybody else?" Some companies succumb to this message.

Then the market turns and things become difficult. The zero-sum gamers become even louder. "The only way to win now is by giving up these stupid, naïve principles of yours, you silly little anarchist." "We need to play the game with the big boys, the professionals, the regulators. We need to do this professionally and legitimately." By legitimately, they mean in a way that they can corrupt over time.

When the professionals come and say, "Let us take over and fix your project," they crush the creative spirit. They will extract everything they can from the carcass of your company, in return for restricted stock units redeemable after a vesting cliff. They will sell your soul in order to have an exit. As soon as the market changes, they will ask you to sell out your principles. So don't sell out your principles. Instead hold on to them.

Built by Amateurs

Welcome to our creative commons, which was built not by professionals, but by amateurs.

Do you know what the root of the word amateur is? It is from the French for *lover of*. An amateur is someone who does something out of love. This space was built by people who love what they do, and who pour their passion and creativity into their work.

Bitcoin and the cryptos that followed were not built by paid professionals. They were not developed by a committee. They were built by naïve, idealistic weirdos with creative tendencies who loved to do this, not because they wanted to make money, but because they wanted to bring hope.

A Festival of the Commons

We are building a beautiful alternative for the world, a creative commons and a festival of innovation. Everything that anyone creates in this entire space enriches other projects. Every drawing or painting, every song and talk, every rebellious meeting in a dank basement that nobody believes is important. Every time you introduce someone else to our industry, to our principles. Even the failures of every shitcoin. It all adds to this ecosystem we share.

This is about building something that gives us hope. Together, we're building our creative commons for the future.

Thank you!

BONUS Canadian Senate Testimony: Opening Statement

On October 8, 2014, Andreas testified before the *Canadian Senate's Committee on Banking, Trade and Commerce* in Ottawa, Canada, as part of their study on the use of digital currency. Video Link: https://aantonop.io/CAsenate

Publisher's note: What follows is the opening statement of expert witness Andreas M. Antonopoulos, who was asked to testify about Bitcoin, open blockchains, and digital currencies. The statement was read into the record and a lengthy question and answer session followed. The entire testimony, including the question and answer portion of the hearing, can be seen at the link above.

Opening Statement

I appreciate the opportunity to contribute to these proceedings about digital currency.

My experience is primarily in information technology and network architecture. I have a Master's degree in networks and distributed systems and have worked in the field since 1992. I spent 20 years working on networks and data centers for financial services companies before I found Bitcoin in late 2011. I have been working full time in the Bitcoin space for the past 2 years and have written a book for software developers with the title *Mastering Bitcoin.*

Today, I welcome the opportunity to talk to you about Bitcoin's security, the decentralized architecture that underpins Bitcoin's security and the implications that architecture has for privacy, individual empowerment, innovation and regulation.

Until the invention of Bitcoin in 2008, security and decentralization seemed like contrary concepts. Traditional models for financial payment systems and banking rely on centralized control in order to provide security. The architecture of a traditional financial network is built around a central authority such as a clearing house. As a result, security and authority have to vest it in that central actor.

The resulting security model looks a series of concentric circles with very limited access to the center and increasing access, as we move further away from the center. However, even the outermost circle cannot afford open access. In such a security model, the system is carefully protected by controlling access and ensuring that only vetted individuals and organizations can connect to it. The entities near the center of a traditional financial network are vested with enormous power, act with full authority and therefore, must be very carefully vetted, regulated and subject to oversight.

Centralized financial networks can never be fully open to innovation because their security depends on access control. Incumbents in such networks effectively utilize access control to stifle innovation and competition, presenting it as consumer protection. Centralized financial networks are fragile and require multiple layers of oversight and regulation to ensure that the central actors do not abuse their authority and power for their own profit. Unfortunately, the centralized architecture for traditional financial systems concentrates power, creating cozy relationships between industry insiders and regulators, and often leads to regulatory capture, relaxed oversight, corruption and in the end, financial crisis.

Bitcoin and other digital currencies based on an open blockchain architecture are fundamentally different. The security model of open blockchain currencies is decentralized. There is no center to the network, no central authority, no concentration of power and no actor in whom complete trust must be vested. Instead, the core security functions are in the hands of the end users of the system. In this architecture, security is an emergent property of the collaboration of thousands of participants in the network, not the function of a single authority. In addition to the difference in architecture, there are also fundamental differences in the nature of payments themselves.

Digital currencies like Bitcoin are much more like cash than bank accounts or credit cards. The transfer of value in Bitcoin is a push mechanism, not a pull mechanism as in the case of credit cards, debit cards, and most other digital payments. A Bitcoin payment is not an authorization to pull from your account. Instead, it pushes the precise payment amount itself as a value token, directly to the named recipient.

A single transaction does not authorize any future transaction or expose the user's identity. The transaction itself is unforgeable and unchangeable. As a result, Bitcoin payments can be transmitted without encryption over any network and can be stored on unsecured systems, without fear of compromise. Bitcoin's unique architecture and payment mechanism has important implications for network access, innovation, privacy, individual empowerment, consumer protection and regulation.

If a bad actor has access to the Bitcoin network, they have no power over the network itself and do not compromise trust in the network. This means that Bitcoin network can be open to any participants without vetting, without authentication or identification, and without prior authorization.

Not only can the network be open to anyone, but it can also be open to any software application again without prior vetting or authorization. The ability to innovate without permission, at the edge of the Bitcoin network, is the same fundamental force that has driven internet innovation for 20 years, at a frenetic pace, creating enormous value for consumers, economic growth, opportunities, and jobs.

Bitcoin's decentralized nature affords consumer protection in the most powerful and direct way, by allowing Bitcoin users direct control over the privacy of the financial transactions. Bitcoin does not force users to surrender identity with every transaction and put their trust in the chain of supposedly vetted intermediaries, who must be trusted to control access to securely store and protect transaction data and vulnerable account identifiers. Bitcoin transactions never expose vulnerable account identifiers. Bitcoin users can protect the privacy of their transactions without relying on, or trusting, any intermediaries.

Because in Bitcoin trust is not vested in central actors, there is no need for centralized regulation and oversight. When properly architected, Bitcoin financial services are not vulnerable to a central point of failure, which would necessitate heavy-handed oversight and regulation. Instead, the power lies with the end user, whose interests are most aligned with the protection of their own funds. While individual Bitcoin wallets can be targeted and compromised if not properly secured, the Bitcoin network does not suffer from centralized systemic risks.

Contrary to popular misconception, Bitcoin is not unregulated. Rather, several aspects of the Bitcoin network and financial system are regulated by mathematical algorithms. The algorithmic regulation in Bitcoin offers users predictable, objective, measurable outcomes, such as a predictable rate of currency issuance. These outcomes are not subject to the whims of centralized institutions or committees, which are both corruptible and often placed outside of democratic oversight. A Bitcoin user can predict the monetary supply 30 years from now, instead of hanging on the tone and nuanced delivery of a single adjective, by some high official of central banking, who can dramatically change an entire country's monetary velocity a week hence.

Bitcoin's decentralized architecture does not easily conform to the expectations and experiences of consumers or regulators because there has never been a large-scale, secure, decentralized network before. The combination of decentralization and security is the novelty at the heart of Bitcoin. Trying to understand consumer protection, oversight, audit and regulation of Bitcoin, there is a risk that many will try to apply familiar models of the past to this new digital currency system. But those models are all centralized and the familiar models are designed to provide regulation oversight of centralized financial networks. Centralized solutions will be easier to understand and seem familiar, however, they are both inefficient and unsuitable for this new form of decentralized financial network.

I urge you to resist the temptation to apply centralized solutions to this decentralized network. Centralizing Bitcoin will weaken its security, dull its innovative potential, remove its most disruptive, yet also most promising features and disempower its users while empowering incumbents. Consumer protection will not be achieved by removing Bitcoin's built-in privacy characteristics. Demanding users identifiers and adding access control mechanisms on top of the Bitcoin network and then, trusting those identifiers to a chain of intermediaries will only replicate the failures of the past, by introducing single points of failure into a network that has none.

We cannot protect consumers by removing their ability to control their own privacy and then asking them to trust it in the same intermediaries who have failed them so many times before. Most failures in Bitcoin security are the results of misguided attempts at centralization and removing control from the users.

In these new decentralized financial networks, we have the opportunity to invent new decentralized security mechanisms. Based upon innovation such as multi-signature escrow, smart contracts, hardware wallets, decentralized audit and algorithmic proofs of reserves. These are the new decentralized regulatory and security tools that are most appropriate for a decentralized digital currency.

Thank you for the opportunity to address this committee.

Link to Senate Report

Publisher's note: The Canadian Senate's Committee on Banking, Trade and Commerce heard from 55 witnesses in all before drafting a comprehensive report on digital currencies. Read the report (last accessed December 5, 2019) by searching for Digital Currency: You Can't Flip This Coin! (June 2015) *available on SenCanada.ca.*

BONUS Interview: Senate Testimony & Mastering Bitcoin

The original interview was conducted with the Bitcoin community in Vancouver, Canada on October 16, 2014 as part of the *Salon Talks* series of Decentral Vancouver. Video Link: https://aantonop.io/SalonTalks

Publisher's note: This interview was conducted just 8 days after Andreas' legendary testimony in front of the Canadian Senate and contains his reflections on both the preparation and delivery of that testimony. In addition, Andreas talks about writing his first book, Mastering Bitcoin. We've included portions of the interview that provide a rare glimpse into what really happens behind the scenes. We hope you enjoy it.

Thank you for that warm introduction but please, call me Andreas; Mr. Antonopoulos is my father. The Canadian Senate hearing was quite exciting; it was my first time in that kind of environment.

Preparing for My Canadian Senate Testimony

At first, I was quite nervous about speaking to this specific audience. I actually spent several days beforehand trying to decide if I was going to wear a suit. I know that sounds like a trivial consideration, but I haven't worn a suit in three years. Ever since I stopped consulting with banks and corporate executives and started doing my own thing, I stopped wearing suits. That's served me pretty well. But considering the audience, I thought a suit was appropriate, so I went for a compromise solution. As you'll see in the video, I was wearing a tie. My tie had a pattern on the front in binary that spelled: "Ties suck." Then, I used that to break the ice.

When the senators came in, I let them know that I wore a tie for the first time in 3 years, but that there was a message in binary on the tie. I told them, "It says ties suck". They found that quite amusing. I didn't want them to think it was a secret message to the community or something like that. Unfortunately, they don't sell ties that say things like "Vires in Numeris" or "To the Moon" so I just went with something simple.

It was kind of interesting because I didn't know what to expect, but when I first went into the room, as the senators started arriving, they were all extremely friendly. They told me that they were really looking forward to the presentation and had been reading the opening remarks. They were all very easy going and very nice to me. It was a very welcoming crowd and I wasn't really expecting that.

I delivered my opening remarks.

I considered reading them in French. Since I speak French and I had the French translation in front of me, but then I thought that everybody on Reddit would just go bezerk if I read it in French. *Audience Laughter*

I decided to cut my losses and didn't do that.

I was pleasantly surprised that the tone of the conversation was very open and welcoming. The senators seemed to be really listening to what I had to say. Keep in mind that I was really trying to speak to three different audiences, simultaneously. My first audience were, of course, the Senators in the room. My second audience were their constituencies, the Canadian people in general who had an interest in Bitcoin and digital currencies who were watching the hearing or who would watch it later. Finally, I was hoping to provide some useful analogies and narratives to explain the basics of Bitcoin and digital currencies that others could use. I was particularly interested in providing those who support deregulation or non-regulation with good arguments to pose in future debates. At the same time, I was keenly aware that every word I said would be scrutinized by the global Bitcoin community. I thought I might receive threats because I paused too long before saying: "Don't regulate" or something like that. Reddit and Twitter can be pretty vicious when it comes to criticism.

I delivered the opening statement. Then, I got the questions. Most of them were interesting, thoughtful questions that allowed us to discuss very important issues. I was a bit concerned when the first question was about terrorism and ISIS. I was hoping that the entire conversation wouldn't be about Bitcoin being a tool for terrorism, which is obviously a ridiculous statement, as you all know. I was pleasantly surprised when we quickly moved on to other topics. At the end of the hearing, the senators came up to me one by one and thanked me for appearing. They all said something nice to me; they were all very welcoming.

One of the senators told me that during my presentation, they were nearly brought to tears by the discussion about the unbanked and the economically disenfranchised people, which I thought was great. Because that's one of the main messages I wanted to talk about, the fact that Bitcoin isn't just for us. In many cases, it's more for the other 6 billion. As I reflect on the experience, I think it was a very successful day. I hope that I represented Bitcoin well to Canada.

Thanks For The Help and Support

Before we move on to the next topic, I would like to say that I had a lot of help in the senate preparation. First of all, I collaborated in advance with both the Bitcoin Embassy of Canada, as well as Bitcoin Decentral in Toronto. I spoke to several members of the local Canadian Bitcoin groups to ask them about concerns, as well as issues that the Canadian Senate was bringing up. The opening remarks were sent in advance to a couple of trusted people in the Canadian Bitcoin community to review. They gave me some feedback which was extremely helpful. I spent the two days before my appearance reading all of the transcripts and catching up on what had already happened and what had been discussed.

In addition, some friends helped me by doing mock debates, where they asked me questions that had come up before in the Senate transcripts, as well as harder questions and more pointed questions and in some cases, very uncomfortable questions. That allowed me to practice various responses. A lot more went on behind the scenes than you might think, a lot of people were involved. While I'm not into sports, for me, this was game night. So, some coaching and some team practice happened in advance of that presentation. I just wanted to make sure that people understood that this wasn't just me. It was a team effort, a lot of people contributed to make it a successful outcome and I'm very grateful for their help.

Let's Talk About Mastering Bitcoin

The book is called *Mastering Bitcoin*. It's a project that I started, it seems like so long ago, in March of 2013. With the help of many people, I put together a proposal. I thought it was important to have a book about Bitcoin, focused for developers. One that would offer developers the opportunity to learn about cryptocurrencies and to study the topic. If you're a developer, then you probably know O'Reilly media. Most developers I know have at least two or three O'Reilly books on their bookshelves. O'Reilly media publishes a series of books called the Safari Series, which have animals on the covers. These are very well known as high-quality technical books. In fact, most of them are known simply by the animal that's on the cover. For example, if you do Pearl, you know the Camel book. If you've done SendMail, you know the Bat, etc.. These books are very useful references and written to help you understand the technologies. When I wrote my book proposal, I had twenty-three O'Reilly books on my bookshelf. So, when it came time to say: "Which publisher do I want to go for?" All I had to do was to look at my bookshelf.

In March of 2013, I started this process. I decided, you know what? I'm going to write the book for Bitcoin, which at the time, was a ridiculously stupid idea. It was a massive overreach on my part because I had been in Bitcoin for just over a year, a year and 3 months. I understood the technology not very deeply, but deeply enough that I could write some software around Bitcoin and I played with it. I'd started a couple of projects that became companies and did some open source projects in Bitcoin. But really, I wasn't an expert at the time. I'd also never written a book at that time.

Mastering Bitcoin is my first book. It was a bit of an audacious project in retrospect, it was the kind of thing that really didn't make sense, had I really thought about how messy it was I wouldn't have published it. If I had known how much work it would be, I would have given up then and saved myself a lot of pain. But I didn't.

I decided I was going to pitch my book idea to O'Reilly. But I knew it had to be good. Really good. So I wrote a 23-page proposal. I mentioned every article I'd ever written. I reached out to every person I knew in the media and publishing industry and I got endorsements from all of them. I submitted the proposal and waited. I later learned that the same day I submitted my proposal, they received three other proposals for books about Bitcoin. I feel very fortunate that they chose mine.

I made two requests in my proposal, which were rather critical, I think, in the development of the book. The first one was picking an animal and the second was asking that the book be open-sourced from the beginning, which is a big part of my ethos.

Why are there bugs on the cover?

Many people don't understand why on earth there are ants on the cover of Mastering Bitcoin. Some people said I should have chosen a honey badger. Which would have made for a funny joke, but it's a pretty insider joke. So, most people would not understand the reference. It would also be slightly too cocky as an animal for this purpose. I chose the leaf cutter ant and I want to explain why.

The leaf cutter ant is a fascinating animal because it creates the largest social structures and communities on the planet, second only to human beings. Ants are social animals, but what's interesting about them is that they form superorganisms. The colony of ants is a superorganism. The leaf cutter ant is a perfect example of a superorganism that exhibits emergent behavior that is far greater than the sum of the individual parts. The individual parts, the little animals, the little insects, the ants, are not very intelligent. They can be simulated on a small circuit. They only have a few thousand neurons. They have very simplistic behavior which is driven by pheromones. Yet, when you put a few hundred thousand ants together in a colony they become an intelligent superorganism.

The reason they cut up leaves is not because they eat leaves. They don't eat leaves. They actually chew them up and then, they ferment them with an enzyme and they make a paste. A bit like beer, mash is made as a precursor to beer or whiskey mash. Then, they feed that paste to aphids. Then, they take the honeydew from aphids and they feed that to the larvae. Leaf cutter ants have domesticated another insect species and farm it like cattle. This is an astonishing function because they're the only species known, outside of humans, who domesticate other any other species and farm them. Not a single ant has this behavior in their DNA. That behavior emerges from a network that's created by each member of that network, following a simple set of rules. But the emergent behavior that is created is super complex.

To me, that expresses Bitcoin. I hope I haven't bored you to death with all this ant talk. But to me Bitcoin is amazing because at its heart it's not a super smart system, or a super smart network. At its heart, it's like a leafcutter ant colony. From a very simple set of mathematical rules followed by every single Bitcoin node in the network, we get this emergent complexity and a super intelligent network that does incredible things. That's why there are leafcutter ants on the cover.

Open Source

I believe very strongly in open sourcing content of all types. Every speech, every presentation I do, every piece of software I write, every article I write, almost everything I do is covered under Creative Common licenses, either CC by or CC by SA. That work is available for anyone to reuse, to read, to mash up and share alike (with proper attribution). The second request I made to O'Reilly was to make the book available under an open license.

In January of 2014, I really started writing. Nine months later, I delivered the final draft. It was all written on GitHub in ASCIIdoc markup language. It's all available online. You can see every single commit and every iteration of the chapters, all of the mistakes I made.

I decided to follow the advice of Ward Cunningham, do you know who that is? His name was actually Howard G. "Ward" Cunningham and he invented Wikis. He was once asked, what's the best way to get the correct answer from the internet? I'm paraphrasing but in essence he answered, "The best way to get a correct answer from the internet, is not to ask a question. It is to post the wrong answer and the internet will smugly correct you." That was the process by which I published my book. I wrote it and I created the narrative, but in many cases I posted the wrong answer and the internet smugly corrected me and the book got a lot better. I have a lot of people to thank for that.

On my website, I sold copies for bitcoin and included an optional fundraiser for charity. The deal was that people could buy a signed copy of the book, with a personal dedication, by adding $5.00 or $10.00 dollars to their shopping cart and I would donate that money to charity. I had to shut it down after 270 copies of the book were sold. I suddenly realized that carpel tunnel syndrome was in my future, if I didn't stop the orders. But I did raise $1700.00 for charity. Thank you to everyone who donated! *Audience Applause*

Anything You Wish You Could Add to the Book?

Oh hell yes. Tons of things didn't make it into the book. I realized something about half way through, I realized that a book is never done. There is no part of the book that I couldn't have written better. There is no part of the book that I wouldn't improve today if I had another 10 months. E.M. Forester said, "A work of art is never finished. It is merely abandoned." That's exactly what happened. At some point, I had to decide that from now on, everything else that I want to include has to wait for the second edition. I had to stop at some point and face the deadline. There will be a second edition if Bitcoin is still around a year from now. I think it will be.

Thank you.

Appendix A. A Message from Andreas

Request for Reviews Thanks again for reading this book. I hope you enjoyed reading it as much as I enjoyed creating it. If you enjoyed this book, please take a minute to visit the book's page on Amazon or wherever you purchased it and leave a review. This will help the book gain greater visibility in search rankings and reach more people who may be learning about bitcoin for the first time. Your honest feedback also helps me make the next book even better.

Thank You I want to take this opportunity to formally thank the community for supporting my work. Many of you share this work with friends, family, and colleagues; you attend events in person, sometimes traveling long distances; and those who are able even support me on the Patreon platform. **Without you I could not do this important work, the work I love, and I am forever grateful.**

Thank you.

Appendix B. Want More?

Download a Free Bonus Chapter If you enjoyed this book and would like to be informed about the next book in the series, get entered into raffles for free copies of books in the series, and keep up with translations and other exciting news, please sign up to Andreas' mailing list.

We will not sell or share the list with anyone and will only use it to occasionally send information directly relevant to this book series and Andreas' recent or upcoming work. As a thank you for signing up, you'll be able to download a FREE bonus chapter that isn't part of any of the other books. The bonus talk is not available for sale; it's available exclusively to mailing list members.

To sign up please scan this:

Or type in this URL:

aantonop.io/tiom3wantmore

The Internet of Money Series, Print, Ebooks, and Audiobooks This book is the third in a series called *The Internet of Money*. If you enjoyed this book, you might also enjoy Volumes One and Two, which are available in print, ebook, and audiobook formats in the U.S., U.K, Europe, Australia, and elsewhere around the world. Volume One has been translated into Spanish, Korean, Russian, Vietnamese, Portuguese, German, and French with more translations to come. Volume Two has been translated into German and will soon be translated into Spanish, with more translations to come.

Volume One Volume One of the Internet of Money Series contains some of Andreas' most popular talks including:

Scaling Bitcoin, Bitcoin Meetup at Paralelni Polis; Prague, Czech; March 2016;

Privacy, Identity, Surveillance and Money, Barcelona Bitcoin Meetup at FabLab; Barcelona, Spain; March 2016;

Infrastructure Inversion, Zurich Bitcoin Meetup; Zurich, Switzerland; March 2016;

Currency as a Language, Keynote at the Bitcoin Expo 2014; Toronto, Ontario, Canada; April 2014;

Elements of Trust: Unleashing Creativity, Blockchain Meetup; Berlin, Germany; March 2016;

And many more!

Volume Two We've heard some people say Volume Two is even better than Volume One! It contains many of Andreas' most prolific and prescient talks:

Blockchain vs Bullshit, Blockchain Africa Conference; Johannesburg, South Africa; March 2017;

Fake News, Fake Money, Silicon Valley Bitcoin Meetup; Sunnyvale, California; April 2017;

Currency Wars, Coinscrum (MiniCon); London, England; December 2016;

Bubble Boy and the Sewer Rat, Draper University; San Mateo, California; October 2015;

Plus Volume Two includes a bonus Question and Answer Section!

Keeping Up with Andreas Find out more about Andreas, including when he is planning to visit your city, on his website at https://www.aantonop.com. You can also follow him on twitter https://www.twitter.com/aantonop and subscribe to his youtube channel at https://www.youtube.com/aantonop.

And of course, Andreas would not be able to do this work without the financial support of community builders through Patreon. Learn more about his work and get early access to videos, participate in a monthly Q&A session, meet Andreas at community builder only events throughout the world, and get behind the scenes content by becoming a community builder at https://www.patreon.com/aantonop.

Appendix C. Video Links

Edited Talks Each of the chapters included in this book are derived from talks delivered by Andreas M. Antonopoulos at conferences and meetups around the world. Most of the talks were delivered to general audiences, yet some were delivered to limited audiences (like students) for a particular purpose.

Andreas is known for engaging with the audience during his presentations, much of the crowd interaction has been cut from the text because so much of it is non-verbal that it doesn't translate well into text. We encourage you to view the original content, if only to get an idea of what it's like to attend one of these events.

All of the videos and many more are available at his website — https://www.aantonop.com and on his youtube channel — aantonop. https://www.youtube.com/user/aantonop. For early access to his latest videos become a patron at https://www.patreon.com/aantonop.

Original Content Links Below you'll find a list of the talks we've included in this text, along with locations, dates, and links to the original content.

Introduction to The Internet of Money

> Internet Days ("Internetdagarna") Conference; Stockholm, Sweden; November 2017; https://aantonop.io/IntroTIOM

Universal Access to Basic Finance

> CryptoCompare Digital Asset Summit; London, England; June 2019; https://aantonop.io/UniversalAccess

Measuring Success: Price or Principle

> The Internet of Money Tour 2018; University College Dublin; Dublin, Ireland; May 2018; https://aantonop.io/MeasuringSuccess

Libre Not Libra: Facebook's Blockchain Project

> The Internet of Money Tour 2019; Scottish Blockchain Meetup; Edinburgh, Scotland; June 2019; https://aantonop.io/LibreNotLibra

Inside Out: Money as a System of Control

> Advanced Digital Innovation Summit; Vancouver, Canada; September 2017; https://aantonop.io/InsideOut

Worse Than Useless

> Baltic Honey Badger Conference; Riga, Latvia; November 2017; https://aantonop.io/WorseThanUseless

Escaping the Global Banking Cartel

> The Internet of Money Tour 2018; Seattle, Washington; November 2018; https://aantonop.io/EscapingCartel

Bitcoin: A Swiss Bank in Everyone's Pocket

> The Internet of Money Tour 2019; Swiss Bitcoin Association; Zurich, Switzerland; June 2019; https://aantonop.io/SwissBank

Unstoppable Code: The Difference Between Can't and Won't

> ETH Denver; Denver, Colorado; February 2019; https://aantonop.io/UnstoppableCode

Picking the Right Blockchain for the Job

> DigitalK Conference; Sofia, Bulgaria; May 2019; https://aantonop.io/PickingBlockchains

Keeping Digital Communities Weird

> Polish Bitcoin Congress (Polski Kongres Bitcoin); Warsaw, Poland; May 2018; https://aantonop.io/KeepingWeird

Crypto-Winter to the North, Crypto-Summer to the South

> Bitcoin Argentina Meetup; Buenos Aires, Argentina; January 2019; https://aantonop.io/CryptoWinter

BONUS Canadian Senate Testimony: Opening Statement

> Canadian Senate's Committee on Banking, Trade and Commerce; Ottawa, Canada; October 8, 2014; https://aantonop.io/CAsenate

BONUS Interview About Senate Testimony & Mastering Bitcoin

Salon Talks; Vancouver, Canada on October 16, 2014; https://aantonop.io/SalonTalks

Index

Printed in Great Britain
by Amazon

59197786R00097